A HAIKU JOURNEY

Bashō's *Narrow Road to a Far Province*

Translated and introduced by
Dorothy Britton

KODANSHA INTERNATIONAL
Tokyo, New York & San Francisco

This is a revised edition, without the photographs or additional haiku, of *A Haiku Journey*, published in 1974 by Kodansha International Ltd.

Published by Kodansha International Ltd., 12-21, Otowa 2-chome, Bunkyo-ku, Tokyo 112 and Kodansha International/USA Ltd., 10 East 53rd Street, New York, New York 10022 and 44 Montgomery Street, San Francisco, California 94104. Copyright © 1974 by Kodansha International Ltd. All rights reserved. Printed in Japan.

LCC 74-24903
ISBN 0-87011-423-9
JBC 0095-787927-2361
First revised paperback edition, 1980
Third printing, 1981

INTRODUCTION

A seashell
Is a Japanese poem
Of seventeen syllables—
Small and formal in shape
But containing an ocean
Of thoughts.

Poetry in microcosm—a world of ideas in three brief lines of verse—was given vibrant life and form by the celebrated pilgrim-poet Bashō, who lived in Japan in the seventeenth century. Bashō was his pen name. It was his third, in fact. His first published verses were signed Munefusa, and a decade later he chose the name Tōsei, which means "Green Peach," in admiration of the Chinese poet Li Po (705–762), "White Plum." It was not until he was thirty-six, an established poet with a following, that he changed his pen name to Bashō.

A pupil brought him a curious plant which had been introduced to Japan from China. It was a kind of plantain, or banana tree, and the poet fell in love with it at once. He was fascinated by its long, broad leaves, "big enough to make a cover for a *koto*." Frayed by the wind, they made him think of the tail of the mythical phoenix or of a green fan torn to shreds in a gale. "I love to sit under my banana tree," he wrote, "and listen to the sound of the wind and rain upon its leaves." He tended his exotic tree and tried to protect it from encroaching vegetation.

> How I hate to see
> Reed shoots, now that I've planted
> A banana tree!

> Neither is the vine
> Of the wild morning glory
> Any friend of mine!

The Japanese name of the plant was *bashō*, and it was not long before his pupils were calling his solitary abode Bashō-an, "Banana Tree Cottage" (literally, "Banana Tree Hermitage"). What more fitting name could he now take for himself too, the poet thought, than that of his beloved tree?

Bashō's surname was Matsuo, and he was born in 1644, the youngest son of the seven children of a samurai in the service of the Lord of Ueno Castle, located midway between Kyoto and Ise Shrine. At nine, Bashō became page and study-companion to the nobleman's eldest son, a delicate boy of eleven who was talented in the composition of poetry. Together they learned the craft of verse from Kigin (1624–1705), a noted Kyoto poet who was a disciple of the great *haikai* master Teitoku (1570–1653). The two boys became devoted friends.

When Bashō was twenty-two, his aristocratic companion and master died. Heartbroken, Bashō was sent on his first pilgrimage—to Mount Kōya to enshrine a lock of his dead friend's hair at the great Buddhist monastery. There, amidst the temples and the tombs, in the depths of the hallowed forest of gigantic cryptomerias, the poet thought deeply about life's transience and *sabi*, the pathos that is inherent in all things but which is especially well mirrored in the cycle of nature. He determined to leave the castle and devote his life to poetry and contemplation. He also wanted to be far from the sight of his master's beautiful young widow, for he secretly loved her and knew no good could come of it.

The young man went to Kyoto where he begged his master's teacher Kigin to take him into his home as servant-disciple. Bashō spent five years in Kyoto, studying Chinese classics and calligraphy as well as poetry. Another sad love affair persuaded him to renounce the world entirely and become a student of Zen. When, in 1672, he followed Kigin to Edo (present-day Tokyo), whither the latter had been summoned by the shōgun, the twenty-eight-year-old Bashō threw himself wholeheartedly into the practice of Zen meditation under the guidance of the priest Butchō.

Bashō's first poems had appeared in print when he was twenty, and by the time he was thirty-six, he had published numerous poems and anthologies and had acquired a devoted coterie of disciples. That year, one of them, a wealthy fish wholesaler named Sampū, gave

Bashō the tiny watchman's lodge on the banks of the Sumida River that came to be known as Banana Tree Cottage. The following year, 1681, Bashō published an epoch-making verse.

> On a leafless bough
> In the gathering autumn dusk:
> A solitary crow!

This verse marks the beginning of Bashō's own distinctive style. There is nothing contrived. No puns. No attempt at wit. Spare and unpretentious, the lines are a quiet, refined observation of nature. Completely objective, this poem projects the dreariness and sadness of an autumn evening and its undertones of old age and death, without explicitly saying so.

Bashō's pure observation of nature, with his profound underlying mysticism, reached its peak with his most famous poem issued five years later (1686) in a collection of his own and his pupils' poems entitled *Spring Days*.

> Listen! a frog
> Jumping into the stillness
> Of an ancient pond!

On the surface, this poem simply presents a beautiful picture complete with sound effects. It carries one, in imagination, to the veranda of a temple in Kyoto, perhaps, overlooking a landscaped garden hundreds of years old with a moss-edged pond. One hears the sudden plop of a frog jumping into the dark water on a still spring afternoon. But the thought processes started by this poem go on and on. The pond could be eternity, God, or the Ultimate Truth about this universe and man. And we, brash mortals with our works and our inventions—each one of us no better than a frog jumping in—make but a moment's splash, and the ripples circle and die away. . . .

Bashō had always admired the "wandering poets" Li Po and Tu Fu of China and Sōgi and Saigyō of Japan and wanted to make his own poetic pilgrimage. He made not one but several journeys in Japan, always taking with him one or two of his disciples. His first, a leisurely peregrination in 1684 to Ise by way of his old home in Ueno, is described in *Nozarashi Kikō*, "A Weather-beaten Journey." Later, he followed the Tone River to the "water town" of Kashima to visit his Zen teacher Butchō, and the resulting volume was entitled *Kashima Kikō*. He also travelled to see the celebrated cherry trees of Yoshino not far from Kyoto when he visited Ueno again and was invited by the son of his late master to attend a cherry-viewing party in the castle grounds.

> Ah! what memories!
> Myriad the thoughts evoked
> By those cherry trees!

In 1687, he visited Mount Kōya for the second time while en route to the beaches of Suma, Akashi, and Waka-no-Ura and wrote *Oi-no-Kobumi*, "Notes from a

Pilgrim's Pack." Bashō then proceeded to Sarashina to view the harvest moon at Mount Obasute, "the Hill Where They Abandoned Old Women," and penned his *Sarashina Kikō*. After the destruction by fire in 1682 of his first beloved Banana Tree Cottage, and although his friends built him a second one, the poet came more and more to feel the vanity of material possessions. Travelling became a way of life for him. He took to the open road in the spirit of Buddhist philosophy in which life itself is a journey—a pilgrim's progress. On his wide-brimmed sedge hat he penned the pilgrim's motto: *Kenkon mujū; dōkō ninin*—literally, "With no home 'twixt heaven and earth; travellers two," meaning "Homeless I wander, in company with God."

Bashō's most famous haiku journey, the longest of the trips, made in 1689 when he was forty-five, was towards Michinoku (often abbreviated to Oku), Honshu's northernmost province, now called Aomori. The trip was a difficult and perilous undertaking, and the poet and his disciple Sora travelled mostly on foot. But then poets like Sōgi (1421–1502) and Saigyō (1118–1190) had trod the same path even centuries earlier. It was his desire to follow in their footsteps that prompted Bashō to set off on his own arduous pilgrimage. He wanted to see for himself the places mentioned in their poems. Other famous poets too had travelled to those remote regions. Some had even been banished there as political exiles.

The journey took Bashō five months, with little

lingering on the way even for the illness that plagued him at times, and his account of it, *Oku-no-Hosomichi*, "The Narrow Road to a Far Province," is the masterpiece of his prose-and-poetry travel diaries.

Bashō had sold his house before he left, setting off into eternity, as it were, and was not really expecting ever to return alive. Now homeless, he passed the two years following his northward pilgrimage sojourning at various summer cottages lent him by disciples. He stayed for months at Genju-an, "the Hermitage of Ephemeral Life" at Ōmi, and then later at Mumei-an, "the Hermitage without a Name" at Ōtsu, both on the shores of beautiful Lake Biwa. He also stayed at Rakushi-sha, "the House of Fallen Persimmons" near Kyoto. And then in 1692 his disciples built him a new Bashō-an in Edo on the banks of the Sumida River, quite near his old cottage, and planted in the garden not one but five banana trees.

In 1694, Bashō set off once more, this time to walk to the southwestern provinces of Japan as far as the great island of Kyushu. But alas, he got no farther than Osaka, where he fell grievously ill of dysentery and died, an old man at fifty. He was buried at a temple adjoining "the Hermitage without a Name" at Ōtsu, whose view of Lake Biwa he had loved so well.

Poetry's shortest fixed form, the haiku, has a unique background. In the exquisitely refined court circles of Japan's Heian period (8–12th centuries), sensitivity to nature and the ability to write poems and instantly quote and recognize classics of Japanese and Chinese poetry were social requirements. At the same time, Heian court life was so circumscribed, and all its aspects so familiar, that explicitness was boorish and conversation came to be a gentle art of understatement and allusion.

It was hardly surprising, then, that the *chōka*, or "long poem," lost in popularity to the *tanka*, or "short poem," in which a wealth of meaning could be suggested in five lines—five lines elegant in shape and rhythm.

> *Mi-chi-no-be ni*
> *Shi-mi-zu na-ga-ru-ru*
> *Ya-na-gi ka-ge*
> *Shi-ba-shi to-te ko-so*
> *Ta-chi-do-ma-ri tsu-re*

(Let me guide your pronunciation. Say the following sentence, sounding only the vowels, and you have the Japanese sounds *a, i, u, e* and *o*. "But he soon set off." As you will notice, Japanese vowels are pronounced as in Italian or Spanish. Consonants resemble English, except that *g* is hard only when it starts a word, i.e., *ga* as a first syllable is pronounced as in "galore," whereas within a word or as a particle it becomes glottal, like the *nga* in "si*nga*ble." Double consonants are each pronounced separately, i.e., the word *hokku* sounds like "hock-coo," and the name Gassan, like "gus-sun." Double vowels are herein represented by single vowels with a macron over them and should be pronounced twice as long. An exception is *i* which is printed twice, e.g., Iizuka.)

In the *tanka* as above, the *shichi-go chō* (the seven-five meter which is to Japanese poetry and drama what Shakespeare's iambic pentameter is to English) is arranged as a triplet (three lines of 5, 7, and 5 syllables) and a couplet (two lines of 7 syllables). Since the syllables are equally accented, the effect is similar to three- and four-foot lines of English spondees. Keats's much-praised line from "Hyperion" begins like the first line of a *tanka*:

Robs not | one light | seed . . .

Yet English has difficulty in keeping strictly to accented syllables. Here is a translation of the above *tanka* maintaining as closely as possible the Japanese meter. The poem is by Saigyō, and Bashō refers to it when he writes about seeing the same weeping willow in the village of Ashino (see page 39).

> On that roadside lea
>   Where pure, crystal waters flowed,
>   Grew a willow tree;
>   For a little while I stayed
>   There and rested in its shade.

Rhyme is a device unsuited to the Japanese language, but in English it helps to suggest the formal elegance achieved in the original by those elements impossible to translate, which the poet James Kirkup so aptly calls "the subtle play of sound and meaning."

A *tanka* is usually not recited, but is sung to tunes from

the old Buddhist chants, and there is always a pause between the triplet and the couplet, like that between the octet and sestet of a Petrarchian sonnet. The *tanka* is now almost always called *waka*, which means "Japanese poem," once a general term for all forms of native Japanese verse.

The intellectual, aesthetic Heian courtiers devised from *waka* a poetic diversion they called *renga*, or "linked verse," in which one person wrote the triplet and another added the couplet. There were also *kusari-no-renga*, "chains of linked verse," a poetic game any number could play. Since the rules were less exacting than for the composition of serious *waka*, verse linking became immensely popular. For many reigns, the enjoyment of poetry was largely confined to court circles, but by the end of the sixteenth century, members of the rising merchant class began to take a lively interest in verse linking, especially the kind that was composed in a lighter vein and came to be called *haikai* (later renamed *renku*).

The starting triplet, the *hokku*, had a special importance and was always composed by the most distinguished person present. There were two principal requirements: the *hokku* had to contain a seasonal word and a *kireji*, or exclamatory "cutting word," such as *ya* (!) or *kana* (how . . . ! what . . . !).

Over the centuries, the poetic images of the Heian and succeeding periods became stylized into little more than so many conventional word combinations that merely needed assembling. Originality all but disappeared. Then Bashō came along. A skillful writer of linked verse, Bashō infused new art and sensitivity into the form, raising it from a mere pastime into the realm of true poetry. But Bashō's greatest contribution was towards making the starting triplet, the *hokku*, an independent poetic form of miniature perfection, later to be renamed haiku.

Haiku and Japanese art have much in common. Like deftly suggestive *sumi* paintings, these short verses are thought-provokers. The haiku poet rarely describes his own feelings, but lets the juxtaposition of his images make us feel his emotions instead. Seemingly objective, a good haiku should rouse in the reader's mind a deeply subjective response and set in motion a world of thoughts. A haiku makes demands. So much is left unsaid that its three brief lines need more than a casual reading. One should try to immerse oneself in the poem and let the images propel one's thoughts to deeper meanings.

Of course, their centuries of conditioning give the Japanese a certain advantage, for the images focused upon in this poetic form rely heavily on traditional responses. *Hana*, literally "flowers" but actually referring to cherry blossoms; *samidare*, the long June rains; *semi*, the cicada with its lonely cry—words like these immediately conjure up for the Japanese a particular and specific mood. Moreover, the cycle of the seasons, of which the Japanese are keenly aware, is the theme upon which Japanese poets have based their variations. A haiku is not a haiku without its season-setting word. A vast number of words are traditionally associated with a particular time of year. But like "cool," a summer word, and "the full moon," always the harvest moon of autumn, many are less than obvious. To aid poets, the *saijiki*, a glossary of seasonal words, is available. Seldom is one made more conscious of the year's seasonal unfolding than in Bashō's account of his May to October poetic pilgrimage.

The Narrow Road to a Far Province is not just an ordinary travel diary interspersed with poems. The poetry is as integral to the book as the prose, and one complements the other. Bashō sometimes even took liberties with fact to achieve a skillful balance in the work as a whole, as well as in the individual sketches, each one of which, as Soryū implies in his Epilogue, is a pearl. How freely Bashō used poetic license became clear with the discovery of Sora's account of the same journey, entitled *Zuikō Kikō*, "A Travel Companion's Journal." Bashō describes sojourns at places where they did not stay; dates are changed; itineraries reversed, as at Matsushima; and for greater effect he makes out that they stumbled on the port town of Ishi-no-Maki quite by chance after losing their way when in fact it was on their itinerary all along. Sora does not tell us what fruit besides melon the "certain person" served them at his hermitage (page 75), but it cannot have been the eggplant of the original, for this vegetable is not eaten raw. Bashō, in the impromptu haiku he composed for his host, obviously chose *nasubi* for its elegant sound and convenient three syllables. In similar vein I chose the rhyming "pear." And who knows? Japan's crisp, juicy, indigenous *nashi*—a sort of pear-apple—may quite possibly have been the very fruit on Bashō's plate!

To me, *The Narrow Road to a Far Province* has the unity of a musical composition with many and varied movements. Like melodies that come and go, thought patterns introduced in one sketch later recur. The last haiku, with its sadness for departing autumn, echoes the theme of departing spring in the haiku with which the journey begins. Major keys are set against minor modes, as in the sketch on page 55 where the description of Zuigan-ji's golden splendor is given an acerbic little coda. Place names are worked into the fabric, as in his ingenious improvisation on the theme of water at Shitomae-no-Seki (page 58). At Sukagawa (page 41), moved by thoughts of long-dead poets, Bashō's laconic prose explodes into florid emotive lines of classical seven-five meter:

> With my soul enthralled
> By the beauty of the scene,
> And my heart pierced through
> Thinking of those bards of yore . . .

It is like a rich, sonorous passage played by full orchestra before the music drops to a solo flageolet in a striking contrast of simplicity with his modest little gem of a haiku. And what a gem it is! With earthy motifs jostling lofty themes, and lyricism contrasted even at times with harsh dissonance, Bashō's gamut of word color resembles a composer's tone palette.

Bashō packs a surprising amount of action into his vignettes. Literary overtones add further counterpoint. Echoes of other poems and stories intertwine the images. But when Bashō plucks a single string that would have set off sympathetic reverberations in the mind of the well-read contemporary, today and in another tongue some further "orchestration" is required. Wherever artistically possible I have filled out Bashō's fleeting allusions to make them meaningful to the English-speaking reader without recourse to tiresome footnotes. I have mostly, but not always, enclosed explanatory passages in brackets.

Bashō's range of expression is multifarious. There are even touches of eroticism in spite of the poet's having renounced the pleasures of the flesh. He contemplates with obvious delight the physical grace of nubile young women's hands busy at their traditional task of transplanting new rice. He betrays an intimate knowledge of how women make themselves beautiful. And he even indulges in an unpriestly preoccupation with the courtesans from Niigata.

The word-economy of haiku in Japanese is aided by the language's many homonyms—words with the same sound but different meanings. For instance, *shinobu*, "hare's foot fern" (page 43), also means "to recollect, or be reminded of." So, while only used once, it has the effect of being used twice: *mukashi shinobu shinobu-zuri*, "I am reminded of the past when they rubbed ferns." The final haiku on page 85 is a tour de force with enough double meanings to make two complete verses. It can be read in the following ways: (1) "Now that it is autumn, I leave you for Futami [short for Futami-ga-Ura], famous for its clams." (2) "As the clam's shell parts from its meat, I go. Autumn goes too." I have put the additional meaning in prose just preceding the haiku.

The title, too, is a tour de force. Bashō borrowed the name of a road he came across in his northbound odyssey (page 49). Laden with meaning, his inspired title is difficult to translate. Some of the word *oku*'s meanings are: "the far recesses, the inner reaches, the hinterland, the interior." *Oku* is also an abbreviation of Michinoku, or Michi-no-Oku, "the road's far recesses"—the popular name for the region known then as Ōshū, "the far provinces." Japanese nouns are at once both singular and plural. In taking *Oku-no-Hosomichi* for his title, Bashō must have had in mind its wider meaning, embracing all the desolate, rugged footways penetrating the remote frontier. The original "Narrow Road" is now a busy thoroughfare in Iwakiri on the outskirts of the bustling city of Sendai. But the eighth-century Tsubo Stone of Taga Castle (page 49), not far from Iwakiri, is still preserved, and besides giving distances to various places it states that hostile Ainu country was then but forty-eight miles away. The poet's title may have philosophical connotations as well, implying that Bashō's journey was also a poetic peregrination into the inner reaches of the mind.

The lunar calendar was used in Japan until the adoption of the Gregorian system in 1872. I have given in brackets the Gregorian equivalent of the lunar dates for the year of Bashō's journey. Most traditional festivals now conform to the modern dating. For example, the Iris, or Boy's Festival (page 48), now permanently falls on the fifth day of today's fifth month.

In translating haiku and *waka* I consider it essential to try and make them seem in English as complete and formal as they are in the original Japanese. To do this, I find the use of some measure of consonance helpful. It has become customary, alas, to render haiku and *waka* in English in free blank verse. To my mind this not only gives them a modern flavor they lack in the original, but too often makes them seem but trivial, formless fragments. Haiku are miniscule, but certainly not fragmentary. They are classical, strictly formal little gems, and this is the impression I have done my utmost to convey across the barrier of language.

The reader may wonder why the three and five lines of haiku and *waka* in the original Japanese are printed in a single continuous line, like prose. This custom apparently began when printing was first introduced, for the sake of economy. Paper was scarce and the carving of the wood blocks time-consuming and expensive.

When writing poetry by hand it is a different matter altogether. Then the visual aspect comes into its own.

In *The Narrow Road to a Far Province* Bashō has quoted two *waka* by earlier poets in their entirety—those by Butchō and Saigyō on pages 37 and 80 respectively. But more often he merely quotes a single line when referring to some well-known poem. I have sometimes taken the liberty of supplying a few more lines—sometimes the whole *waka*—in order to enhance the reader's understanding and pleasure. Professor Hirō Nakano's comprehensive notes in the 1973 Nichieisha edition of *Oku-no-Hosomichi* have been of inestimable help to me in translating Bashō's work. I am also indebted to the late Professor Asatarō Miyamori's *An Anthology of Haiku: Ancient and Modern* (Maruzen, 1932) for some of the biographical and historical information, and to Mr. Nobuyuki Yuasa's *The Narrow Road to the Deep North and Other Travel Sketches* (Penguin Classics, 1970) for English spellings of Chinese names; and also to the Royal Horticultural Society for help with the names of plants.

Dorothy Guyver Britton
(Lady Bouchier)
Hayama, December 1979 (revised)

BASHŌ'S ROUTE

JAPAN SEA

Sado Is.

Noto Peninsula

Nago Beach
Ichiburi Barrier
Kurobe R.

KANAZAWA

Daishōji
Komatsu
Yoshizaki
Maruoka
Yamanaka Spa
FUKUI
Eihei-ji
Shirane-ga-Take
(Hakusan)
Mt. Hino

Iro-no-hama

Tsuruga

ŌGAKI

L. Biwa

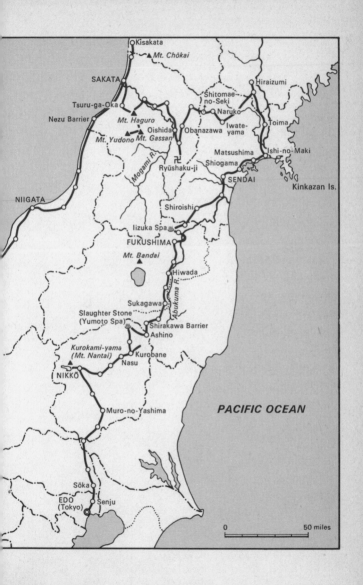

Kisakata

▲ Mt. Chōkai

SAKATA

Tsuru-ga-Oka

Nezu Barrier

Mt. Haguro

Oishida

Mt. Yudono Mt. Gassan

Mogami R.

Ryūshaku-ji

NIIGATA

Shitomae-
no-Seki

Naruko

Obanazawa

Iwate-
yama

Matsushima

Shiogama

SENDAI

Hiraizumi

Toima

Ishi-no-Maki

Kinkazan Is.

Shiroishi

Iizuka Spa

FUKUSHIMA

Mt. Bandai ▲

Hiwada

Abukuma R.

Sukagawa

Slaughter Stone
(Yumoto Spa)

Shirakawa Barrier

Ashino

*Kurokami-yama
(Mt. Nantai)*

Kurobane

Nasu

NIKKŌ

Muro-no-Yashima

PACIFIC OCEAN

Sōka

EDO
(Tokyo)

Senju

0   50 miles

THE NARROW ROAD
TO A FAR PROVINCE

☽ Prologue

The passing days and months are eternal travellers in time. The years that come and go are travellers too. Life itself is a journey; and as for those who spend their days upon the waters in ships and those who grow old leading horses, their very home is the open road. And some poets of old there were who died while travelling.

There came a day when the clouds drifting along with the wind aroused a wanderlust in me, and I set off on a journey to roam along the seashores. I returned to my hut on the riverbank last autumn, and by the time I had swept away the cobwebs, the year was over.

But when spring came with its misty skies, the god of temptation possessed me with a longing to pass the Barrier at Shirakawa, and the road gods beckoned, and I could not set my mind to anything. So I mended my breeches, put new cords on my hat, and as I burned moxa on my knees to make them strong, I was already dreaming of the moon over Matsushima.

I sold my home and moved into Sampū's guest house, but before I left my cottage I composed a verse and inscribed it on a poem strip which I hung upon a pillar:

This rude hermit cell
  Will be different now, knowing Dolls'
    Festival as well.

🐚 Setting Forth

On the twenty-seventh day of the Third Moon [May 16], the dawn sky was misty. There was a wan moon, and in the faint morning light I could just make out, in the distance, the summit of Fuji and, nearby, the tops of the cherry trees of Ueno and Yanaka. Would I ever see these sights again, I wondered, feeling rather forlorn.

My closest friends, who had been with us since the night before, came on the riverboat to see us off. We disembarked at a place called Senju, and my heart was heavy at the thought of the miles that lay ahead. And though this ephemeral world is but an illusion, I could not bear to part from it and wept.

  Loath to let spring go,
    Birds cry, and even fishes'
      Eyes are wet with tears.

I composed this verse as a beginning to my travel diary, and we set off, but our feet dragged and we made little progress. Our friends stood on the road and watched us until we were out of sight.

✿ Sōka

Here am I, in the Second Year of Genroku [1689], suddenly taking it into my head to make a long journey to far, northern provinces. I might as well be going to the ends of the earth! There will be hardships enough to make my hair white, but I shall see with my own eyes places about which I have only heard! I shall be fortunate if I but return alive, I thought, staking my future on that uncertain hope. We finally arrived later that day at the post town of Sōka.

What I find most trying is carrying my belongings on my thin, bony shoulders. I set out thinking to travel light, in only what I was clad, but I needed a durable paper coat to keep out the cold at night, a cotton kimono, rainwear, and such things as ink and brushes. Then there were various farewell gifts I could not refuse and cannot very well throw away, so these are burdens I shall have to bear.

We visited the Shrine of the Burning Bower at Yashima. Said my travelling companion Sora:

"The deity enshrined here is Konohana Sakuya Hime, the Goddess of Flowering Trees, who is also enshrined on Mount Fuji. This holy place is called the Shrine of the Burning Bower because when the deity's god-husband refused to believe that the child she conceived on their single night together was his, the goddess walled herself up in a lying-in bower of wattle and daub and set fire to herself, declaring that if her infant were born unharmed, it would prove her innocence. The son she bore was the god Hohodemi, or 'the Flame-born.' When writing poetry here it is therefore customary to make some reference to smoke."

Apparently there are various other traditions observed here too, such as not eating a fish called *konoshiro* which, when grilled, smells like human flesh burning.

🐑 Hotoke Gozaemon

On the thirtieth day of the Third Moon [May 19], we stayed the night at the foot of Mount Nikkō. The innkeeper said:

"I'm known as Saintly Gozaemon. I put honesty first in all matters, and that is why people call me that. You may sleep soundly tonight, with total confidence."

We wondered which saint had taken human form in this wicked world to look after two beggar pilgrims in priestly garb. As we carefully observed the innkeeper, we saw that he was utterly devoid of worldly wisdom or self-interest and that he was stubbornly honest to a fault. How closely he approached the Confucian ideal of *gōki bokutotsu*, "strength of character and rugged honesty"! A person like that is to be esteemed highly.

☽ Nikkō

On the first day of the Fourth Moon [May 20], we paid
our respects at Mount Nikkō.

In olden times, the name of this mountain was written
"Ni-kō," using the Chinese characters for "two" and
"wild," but when Saint Kūkai built a temple here, he
changed the characters to "Nik-kō," meaning "sun"
and "light." He must have foreseen what was to come a
thousand years later, for now the august light of the
Tokugawa rule illumines the whole firmament, and its
beneficent rays reach into every corner of the land so
that all the people may live in security and peace.

I was filled with such awe that I hesitated to write a
poem.

> O holy, hallowed shrine!
>> How green all the fresh young leaves
>>> In thy bright sun shine!

Kurokami-yama, which means "Mount Raven
Locks," though wreathed in spring mists, was still white
with snow. Sora composed a verse:

> With my hair clean shorn,
>> I came to Mount Raven Locks
>>> On Garb Changing Morn.

Sora is his pen name. His surname is Kawai and he
is called Sōgorō. He lived near Banana Tree Cottage
and used to help me with household chores. Sora was

delighted at the prospect of seeing the views at Matsu-shima and Kisakata and came with me to keep me company and share the rigors of the road. He shaved his head the morning we left, changed into a priest's black robe, and took the Buddhist name of Sōgo (Religious Enlightenment). His verse composed at Mount Kurokami refers to this. The words "Garb Changing" are very effective, meaning both the day when one changes into summer clothing and Sora's own "garb changing" when he took religious vows before coming on this journey.

A mile or so up the mountain was a waterfall. The water seemed to take a flying leap and drop a hundred feet from the top of a cave into a green pool surrounded by a thousand rocks. One was supposed to sidle into the cave and enjoy the falls from behind, hence its name Urami-no-Taki, "the Waterfall Viewed from Behind."

> There we did begin,
> Cloistered in that waterfall,
> Our summer discipline.

I knew someone who lived in a place called Kurobane in the Nasu district, so we decided to cross Nasu Moor. We took a shortcut in the direction of a village we could see far off in the distance, but before we reached the village, it began to rain and night came on. We spent that night at a farmhouse and the next morning started off again across the moor.

We came upon a horse grazing. Nearby, a man was

cutting grass and we inquired the way. Although he was a country fellow, he was not lacking in kindness.

"Dear me!" he said, concerned. "This moor be all a tangle of paths, and a stranger could easily go astray. Take my horse and when he will go no farther, send him back."

He lent us his mount. No sooner had we set off than two children came running after us. One was a little girl who said her name was Kasane, which means "Manifold." It was such an unusual and charming name that Sora composed the following lines:

> Were she a flower,
>> She would be a wild, fring'd pink,
>>> Petals manifold.

Before long we reached a small hamlet of a few dwellings, and so, tying some money to the saddle, we let the horse find his own way back.

Kurobane

We visited a man by the name of Jōbōji, who was looking after the manor house of the Lord of Kurobane. He was overjoyed at our unexpected arrival, and we talked all day and through most of the night. His younger brother Tōsui danced attendance upon us from morning till night and even invited us to his own home, as well as taking us to meet his relatives.

During our stay, we took a walk to the outskirts of the town. There we saw the remains of a stockade where, in ancient times, men on horseback practiced archery by aiming blunted arrows at running dogs. Then, wending our way through Nasu's much-sung field of bamboo grass to the old tumulus of Lady Tamamo, we went on from there to visit a shrine dedicated to Hachiman, the God of Battle. When I heard it was this very shrine whose deity was invoked by Yoichi of Nasu when he cried, "Hachiman, O Guardian God of my native land!" as he aimed his desperate arrow at the fan suspended from the tossing enemy boat, my heart stirred within me. It began to get dark, so we returned to Tōsui's house.

There was also a temple there of the Buddhist Shugen sect, called Kōmyō-ji. We were taken to it and said a prayer before the image and the high wooden clogs of the founder, En the Ascetic, who is said to have traversed these hills in those very clogs, preaching.

In the hills, 'tis May.
Bless us, holy shoes, as we
Go upon our way!

✨ Ungan-ji

Behind a temple called Ungan-ji, which is not far from Kurobane, my Zen mentor, the priest Butchō, once had his monastic retreat. I remember him saying he had inscribed the following poem in pinewood charcoal on a rock:

> Scarcely five feet wide,
>> And no more than five feet high,
>>> Is my humble cell.
> Yet I'd need no hut at all,
> Were it not for rains that fall.

Wanting to see what remained of the retreat, I inclined my staff towards the temple of Ungan-ji. A group of friends from Kurobane wanted to come too. There were many young people, and we had such a jolly time along the way, we reached the foot of the mountain before we knew it.

A path disappeared up a valley amidst a dark forest of pines and cryptomerias. Dew dripped from the moss, and though it was early summer, the air was cold. At the end of a picturesque approach called "the Ten Views," we crossed a bridge and passed through the two-tiered temple gate.

Wondering where to find the site of the retreat, we clambered up a hill behind the temple and saw a tiny hut built atop a rock and propped against a small cave. It looked for all the world like Yuan-miao's cave, "Death's

Gate," in China or Fa-yun's rock-top retreat.

> Woodpecker! 'tis well
> You harm not this hermitage
> In its summer dell!

I hastily penned these lines and left the verse hanging on a post of the hut.

🐗 Sesshōseki, or "the Slaughter Stone"

We returned to Kurobane and from there we went to see the Slaughter Stone of Nasu. [According to legend, when Lady Tamamo, loved by Emperor Konoe (r. 1139–1155), was found to be a fox in human guise and was put to death, her fox-soul turned itself into this noxious stone.]

The lord's caretaker, my friend Jōbōji, lent us horses for the excursion. The man leading my horse asked me for a poem. What an artistic request for a stablehand to make, I thought, and composed the following verse for him:

> Turn across that moor,
> O horseman, for I hear
> A cuckoo singing there!

The Slaughter Stone was in a mountain niche where

there was a hot spring. The stone's poisonous vapors were as yet unspent, and bees and moths lay dead all around in such heaps that one could not see the color of the sand beneath.

◖ Saigyō's Willow at Ashino

The poet Saigyō's weeping willow that grew "Where pure, crystal waters flowed" was in the village of Ashino. There we found it, still growing on a bank between rice paddies.

Lord Ashino had often urged me to see this willow, and I used to wonder about it. And now, there I was, actually standing in the shade of that very tree!

> One whole paddy field
>> Was planted ere I moved on
>> From that willow tree!

◖ The Barrier at Shirakawa

It was not until we finally reached the checkpoint, or barrier, at Shirakawa that we felt we were really on our way at last. How well I could understand the poet-traveller of days gone by, Taira-no-Kanemori, who felt here that he wanted to send a message "Somehow, to the capital."

Of the Three Great Barriers, this one in particular has always appealed to poets. I loved the trees in their summer green, though I could almost hear the poet Nōin's "Autumn winds ablowing" and see Minamoto Yorimasa's "Crimson maple leaves." The white mantle of snowflowers and wild rambler roses made me think of poets who passed here in the snow.

One ancient hero, writes Kiyosuke, straightened his helmet as he passed this barrier and donned new robes.

> Through the barrier gate
> We passed, with gay snowflowers
> For our new attire!

☆ Sukagawa

After passing the barrier, we crossed the Abukuma River. On our left rose the lofty peak of Mount Bandai, in the region called Aizu, and on our right lay the districts of Iwaki, Sōma, and Miharu, and the range of hills dividing them from Hitachi and Shimotsuke. We passed a place called Kagenuma, or "Mirror Marsh," but that day the sky was clouded over and there were no reflections.

At the post town of Suk'agawa, we called on the poet Tōkyū, and he insisted we spend four or five days with him. The first thing he asked me was, "What were your poetic impressions of the Barrier at Shirakawa?"

"After the rigors of the long journey," I replied, "I was weary in body and spirit, and with my soul enthralled by the beauty of the scene, and my heart pierced through thinking of those bards of yore, I had little inclination for composing poetry.

> For verse, it did suffice
> To hear the northern peasants sing
> As they planted rice.

That was all I wrote. After all, I could hardly pass that barrier without writing a single line."

Using my triplet as a beginning, we took turns and composed three sets of linked verse.

Not far from this post town, in the shade of a huge chestnut tree, lived a priest in seclusion from the world. The quietness and solitude of his retreat reminded me of Saigyō's poem:

> Deep amid the hills,
> Let me sip the pure water
> Of clear mountain rills
> While gath'ring horse chestnuts where
> They are fallen here and there.

I took out some paper and jotted down the following:

"The ideograph for 'chestnut' means 'western tree,'

and people say the chestnut tree has some connection with Buddha's Paradise in the West. Saint Gyōki, throughout his life, used chestnut wood for his staff and for the pillars of his dwellings."

> People of this world
>> Notice not its modest blooms—
>> The chestnut by the eave.

🐏 Asaka Marsh

Only twelve miles from Tōkyū's house was a town called Hiwada. Not much farther on and quite near the road rose the Asaka Hills. The land was very marshy there. It was nearing the season for gathering sweet flags, so we asked a number of people which plant was the *katsumi*, but no one seemed to know. [When the poet Fujiwara-no-Sanekata was exiled here he used *katsumi* for the Iris Festival.] We searched around the marsh, asking people, and while we were walking about repeating over and over "*Katsumi? Katsumi?*" the sun went down behind the hills.

Turning right at Twin Pines, we stopped briefly to see the cave at Kurozuka and went on to Fukushima where we spent the night.

⤳ The Shinobu Mottling Stone

The next day, we went to the village of Shinobu to see the stone against whose rough, naturally patterned surface textiles had been mottled long ago by rubbing fronds of *shinobu*, or hare's foot fern, over the cloth.

In a tiny hamlet at the foot of a distant hill, we found the stone, half-buried in the earth. Some village children came and told us that the stone used to be at the top of the hill, but people going to see it kept pulling up barley to try their hand at rubbing, and the farmers were so annoyed that they dislodged the stone and sent it rolling down into the valley. The children said the stone now lay face down. Their story was quite probably true.

> Young hands planting rice!
> Erstwhile I see them rubbing
> Ferns with equal grace!

⤳ The Site of the Satōs' Maruyama Castle

Crossing the river by the Tsuki-no-Wa (Moon Halo) ferry, we reached the post town of Se-no-Ue (Above the Rapids). The Satō Castle ruins were said to be near the hills about three and a half miles to our left. We were told to go to Saba Moor near the village of Iizuka, and as we went in that direction, frequently asking our way, we came to a spot called Maruyama (Round Hill). It was upon this hill that the famous warriors' castle once stood. We were directed to the foot of the hill, where the sight of the foundation stones of the Great Gate moved us deeply.

In the grounds of an old temple nearby were the tombstones of the Satō family. I was particularly affected by that of the two young brides of the Satō brothers. Battle-widowed, they donned their husbands' heavy armor for the sake of their mother-in-law who had longed to see her sons ride home victorious. The gallant gesture of those gentle women will never be forgotten, I mused, wetting my sleeve with tears. One did not have to travel to far-off China to see the "Weeping Tomb," for here, before this very stone, who could refrain from shedding tears?

We entered the temple and requested tea. Among the temple treasures were Yoshitsune's sword and the wicker travelling chest that Yoshitsune's companion Benkei carried on his back.

> What a proud display!
> Chest and sword and paper carp,
> For Boy's Festival day.

I composed this verse since it was the first day of the Fifth Moon [June 18] and nearing the festival.

☆ Iizuka

We stayed that night at Iizuka. There were hot springs there. After bathing in the waters, we found a place to stay, but it only had straw matting laid upon an earthen floor and was a poor, wretched place. There was not even a lamp, so we chose a place to sleep where there was some light from the hearth and lay down.

That night there was thunder and a heavy downpour, and the roof leaked just above the place where we were lying. What with the fleas and mosquitoes, sleep was impossible. On top of that, my old complaint started up again, and I really thought I was about to breathe my last.

When the short summer night was finally over and it began to get light again, we started on our journey once more. But the night's agony remained, and my spirits were low. We hired horses to take us as far as the town of Kōri.

Having such a long way yet to go, I was filled with misgivings to think I might be taken ill again. But though I might die on the road—on this journey to far and remote places off the beaten track—I was resigned from the beginning to the evanescence of human existence; and if I fall by the wayside and die in a ditch like a beggar, it will merely be my fate. As I mused thus, I gradually regained my spirits a little and was able to tread the earth with firm and resolute steps, and we passed through the Great Gate of Date quite jauntily.

Kasashima

Passing the castle towns of Abumizuri and Shiroishi we entered the province of Kasashima. "Where is the grave of the tenth-century poet, General of the Imperial Guard, Fujiwara-no-Sanekata?" we asked. We were told that at the foot of the hills far off to the right were the villages of Minowa and Kasashima. There we would find the road god's shrine before which Sanekata failed to dismount, and the grave where he was buried after being fatally thrown from his horse in consequence.

Pampas grass yet grew on the tumulus, still "His only memorial," as the poet Saigyō wrote. Because of the rains the road was very bad, and I was weary in body, so we merely gazed at the shrine and grave mound from a distance as we passed.

How appropriate in these June rains were the names Minowa, which means "Straw Raincoat Circle," and Kasashima, "Straw Rain Hat Isle." With this in mind, I wrote the following verse:

> Rain Hat Isle I'd fain
> See, but for the road, alas,
> Muddy with June rain!

We stayed that night at Iwanuma, "Rocky Marshes."

☽ The Takekuma Pine

I simply could not believe my eyes when I saw the famous Takekuma Pine. Just as in olden times, the tree rose from the earth, divided into twin trunks. I thought of the tenth-century poet-priest Nōin. A new governor of the province of Mutsu had cut the tree down and used it for the piers of a bridge across the Natori River, and Nōin wrote, "No trace there is of that pine now." But I had heard that each time a pine was cut down there, a new one had been planted. This one looked as if it had been growing a thousand years. What a splendid and beautiful tree it was!

When I left Edo, Kyohaku composed for me the following verse as his parting gift:

> Though in thy decline,
> Late cherry, show my master
> Takekuma's Pine!

So I wrote the following for him as a reply:

> Since late cherries bloomed,
> I've longed to see the Double Pine—
> Even these three moons!

✿ Sendai

We crossed the Natori River and entered the town of Sendai. It was the fourth day of the Fifth Moon, the eve of the Iris Festival, when fragrant stalks of sweet flag are placed under the eaves for good health. We found an inn and stayed several days.

There was an artist in Sendai by the name of Kaemon. We had heard he was something of a poet and we became friends. Kaemon told us there were many places nearby mentioned in poetry, traces of which had almost disappeared, but which he had found after much searching. One day he took us to see some of them.

Bush clover grew so luxuriantly on Miyagi Moor that I could imagine how beautiful it must be in the autumn. At Tamada, Yokono, and Azalea Hill, the lily of the valley bushes were in full bloom. We walked through a pine forest so thick that the rays of the sun could not penetrate at all. The place was aptly called Kinoshita, "Underwood." The dew must have been heavy there even in ancient times, for, says one old poem:

> Servant, tell thy lord
>   To don his straw rain hat there.

Before the day ended, we also visited such places as a temple dedicated to Yakushi, the Physician of Souls, and a Tenjin shrine.

Kaemon gave us parting gifts of drawings he had made of various places in Matsushima and Shiogama.

He also gave us each a pair of straw sandals with thongs dyed dark blue. His artistic gifts revealed that he was indeed a poet.

> Sandal thongs of blue:
>   We'll seem shod with irises
>   Of the bravest hue!

✼ The Tsubo Stone

Using Kaemon's drawings as our guide, we found ourselves on a road called Oku-no-Hosomichi, "the Narrow Road to a Far Province," which wound along the foot of some hills. We saw the place where the famous sedge of Tofu grows, so often mentioned in poetry. Even now, each year, this reed is plaited into mats and presented to the lord of the manor.

The Tsubo Stone stands on the site of Taga Castle in the village of Ichikawa. The stone is over six feet high and about three feet wide. It was covered with moss, and the inscription was difficult to read. After giving the mileage of the provincial boundaries, it stated: "This castle was built in the First Year of Jinki [724] by General Azuma-Udo, Lord of Ono, who was sent to the Northern Provinces by His Majesty. It was repaired in the Sixth Year of Tempyō-hōji [762] by Imperial Councillor, General Asakari, Lord of Emi, Governor of the

Northeastern Provinces. The first day of the Fifth Moon." The Jinki era was part of the reign of Emperor Shōmu [724–749].

Of all the many places mentioned in poetry, the exact location of most is not known for certain. Landslides have changed the course of rivers, obliterating roads and burying monuments, and trees have grown old and withered away, with young ones taking their place, so that the face of the land is changed and the whereabouts of many famous places is now obscure. But here there is no mistake. This monument was made a thousand years ago and is a very real and vivid link with the past. Seeing it is one of the things that has made my trip worthwhile and one of the happiest moments of my life. Forgetting all the trials of the journey, I wept for sheer joy.

Sue-no-Matsuyama

After that, we visited places made famous by poetry, such as the Tama Brook at Noda and the great stone called Oki-no-Ishi, in the middle of a lake. On Sue-no-Matsuyama, "The Last Pine Hill," there was a temple. The characters in its name were the same as for the hill, but were pronounced "Masshōzan." Among the pine trees were nothing but graves.

Lovers may swear to be forever true, and like two birds with but one pair of wings, or like two trees with branches intertwined as one, be joined together and inseparable, but at the last, they come to this, I mused. I was filled with a great sadness which stayed with me and was made all the deeper by the sound of a temple bell we heard that evening on Shiogama shore.

The June rains had cleared a little, there was a faint moon, and we could see Magaki Isle quite close by. Groups of fishermen were sculling their small boats shorewards, and we could hear the sound of their voices as they divided the catch. I knew then what the poet had in mind when he wrote of "The mooring rope's sad sound."

That night we heard a blind priest playing the lute and singing a narrative song peculiar to this northern region. It was neither like the "Ballad of the Heike Warriors" nor like a dance ballad, but was a country style of music sung in such a loud voice and so near where we were sleeping that we found it very noisy. All the same, I could not help marvelling that such old poetic ballads were still sung here in this remote place.

꩜ Shiogama

Early the next morning, we visited Shiogama Shrine,

rebuilt by Masamune, Lord of Date, when he was governor of the province. The fine wooden pillars were of impressive girth, and the rafter beams were brightly painted. The shrine was at the top of a long flight of stone steps, and its vermilion lacquered fence was brilliant in the morning sunlight. How wonderful it is in this land of ours, I thought, that even in remote and unfrequented places such as this, the divine power of the gods is omnipresent.

In front of this Shinto shrine was an old stone lantern. On its metal casement were the words "Donated by Izumi-no-Saburō in the Third Year of Bunji [1187]." Five hundred years ago, I marvelled! Saburō of Izumi combined the virtues of bravery, integrity, loyalty, and love for his parents. There is no person today who does not revere that glorious name. Truly it has been said: "To him who walks a straight path, true to what he feels is right, honors will come in due time."

Matsushima

It was almost noon, so we hired a boat and set out towards the pine-clad isles of Matsushima. After going about five miles across the water, we finally landed on the beach of Ojima.

It has been said too many times already, but Matsushima is indeed the most beautiful place in all Japan! It can easily hold its own with Lake Tung-ting and Lake Si in China. Open to the sea on the southeast, the bay is over seven miles wide and brims with water, like China's Tsien-tang River.

There are countless islands: some tall, like fingers pointing to heaven; some lying prostrate on the waves; some grouped together in twos and threes, branching to the left or stretching to the right; some with babes upon their backs or clasped to their bosoms, like parents and grandparents.

The pines are a deep, dark green. Their branches are bent by the salt sea winds into naturally graceful shapes, and they have a profound elegance, like that of a beautiful woman whom artifice has made even lovelier still.

Were these islands created by the Great God of the Mountains, in the distant Age of the Gods? Ah! who could possibly do justice with his brush to this wondrous divine work of the Creator of the Universe or presume to describe it adequately in words!

Ojima (Male Island), with its strand jutting way out into the sea, was in fact joined to the mainland. There we saw the site of the Zen priest Ungo's retreat and the stone upon which he used to meditate. Among the pines, we occasionally came across a hideaway where someone lived in seclusion from the world. The peace and tranquillity of one such hermitage, with smoke from pine needles and pinecones rising from its thatch, so attracted us that we called upon its owner though we knew him not. While we were there, the moon came out and shone upon the water, presenting quite a different aspect from the daylight view.

Returning to Matsushima beach, we found an inn with an upper story and wide, open windows looking out to sea. We spent that night "one with the wind and clouds," and with nature's beauty all around us it was a singularly exquisite sensation.

> To the Pine Tree Isles,
> You would need crane's wings to fly,
> Little cuckoo bird!

Sora composed this verse. I wrote nothing and tried to sleep but could not. When I left my old hermitage, Sodō composed a poem for me in Chinese about Matsushima, and Hara Anteki gave me a *waka* containing the line, "Isles with pines upon their shores." I took them out of my bag for company. I had some *hokku*, too, composed for me by Sampū and Jokushi.

☆ Zuigan-ji

On the eleventh day of the Fifth Moon [June 28], we visited Zuigan-ji. Its abbot was the thirty-second in succession since the founding of the temple by Heishirō of Makabe upon his return from China.

Later, the temple was completely rebuilt, commemorating the great virtue of the Zen priest Ungo. With its walls of gold leaf and its resplendent ornaments, it shone with light like paradise itself.

But it was Saint Kembutsu's small temple retreat I really wanted to see.

🐑 Ishi-no-Maki

On the twelfth day of the Fifth Moon [June 29], we set off for Hiraizumi by way of places we had read about in poems, such as Aneha-no-Matsu (Big Sister Pine) and Odae-bashi (Thong-breaking Bridge), but the way seemed little used save by hunters and woodcutters. Not knowing where we were, we lost our way and eventually arrived at a port town called Ishi-no-Maki.

Far across the water we could see the island of Kinkazan, for whose mine "Where flowers of gold blossom" a poet had once felicitated an emperor. Hundreds of boats filled the harbor, and the land was crowded with houses, from every one of whose kitchens smoke was rising.

There we were, purely by chance! We looked for somewhere to stay, but could not find an inn. We finally spent the night at a small and very humble cottage, and as soon as it was light we started off again on unknown roads, often losing our way.

Passing places well known to us through poetry—the ford at Sode, Obuchi Meadow, and the pampas moor of Mano—we followed an embankment that stretched interminably. With sinking hearts, we skirted a long, narrow bog, and we had to spend the night at a place called Toima. We finally reached Hiraizumi the next day. We must have walked about fifty miles.

☽ Hiraizumi

The glory of three generations of Fujiwaras is now but a brief-remembered dream. We reached the ruins of the Great Gate about two and a half miles before we came to the site of Hidehira's manor, where now there were only rice paddies and empty fields. Nothing remained but Kinkeizan, "Golden Pheasant Hill," which was once part of the landscaped gardens.

We climbed up to the Takadachi, Yoshitsune's "High Fort," and saw below us the great Kitagami River which flows from Nambu Province. A tributary, the Koromo River, flows round Izumi Castle and joins the Kitagami here, below the fort. Yasuhira's stronghold stood beyond the Koromo Barrier in a strategic position to guard the entrance to Nambu Province and defend it against the Ainu tribesmen of the north.

But what a fleeting thing is military glory. That select band of loyal retainers who entrenched themselves here in this High Fort and fought so desperately—their glorious deeds lasted but a moment, and now this spot is overgrown with grass. How true the Chinese poet Tu Fu's words:

> Even though a country is defeated,
>   Its mountains and rivers remain.
> And o'er the castle ruins, when it is spring,
>   The grass will be green again.

We sat down upon our straw hats and wept, oblivious of the passing time.

> A mound of summer grass:
>   Are warriors' heroic deeds
>   Only dreams that pass?

> White snowflowers there
>   Remind me of brave old warrior
>   Kanefusa's hair.

Sora

Chūzon-ji's two main halls, which I had heard about for so many years with wonder, were both open to public view. In the temple's Sutra Hall were the statues of the three great frontier generals, and in the Hall of Light were enshrined their coffins and the Buddhist images sacred to their spirits.

The Hall of Light's enamel decoration would have

been scattered long ago and lost—the gem-studded doors shattered by the winds, the gold leaf on the pillars decayed by frost and snow, and the hall itself reduced to a pile of rubble in an empty field of grass—had it not been encased by four new walls and covered over with roof tiles to protect the building from the elements. Thus, it will probably stand for a long time as a memorial of a thousand years ago.

> All June's rainy days
>   Have left untouched the Hall of Light
>   In beauty still ablaze.

Shitomae-no-Seki, or "Passwater Barrier"

The road to Nambu went on, invitingly, even farther north, but we reluctantly turned and retraced our steps to Iwate Village where we spent the night. The next day, passing poetry's Oguro-zaki, "Small Black Promontory," and Mizu-no-Ojima, "the Islet in Midstream," we reached Passwater Barrier. When Yoshitsune's wife gave birth as they fled north together, this was where the newborn babe first passed water. We had come by way of the hot spring at Naruko (Crying Baby).

We planned to cross over the mountains into Dewa

Province. Ours was a road used by few travellers, and the gatekeeper regarded us with much suspicion, but finally allowed us to go on.

Night overtook us in the mountains, but we found the house of a border guard and asked for shelter. A storm marooned us there for three days, and our mountain sojourn was a miserable one.

> Fleas and lice did bite;
>   And I'd hear the horse pass water
>   Near my bed at night.

☆ Natagiri Toge, or "Hatchet-cleft Pass"

According to our host, to get to Dewa Province we would have to cross high mountains. The path was hard to follow so he recommended that we hire a guide. "Then let us do so," we said, agreeing to his suggestion.

Our guide, a young man of magnificent physique who wore a curved dagger in his belt and carried an oak staff, led the way. "This is the day we will surely meet with misadventure," I thought uneasily as we followed him.

Just as our host had forewarned, the mountains were high, and they were so deeply wooded that we heard not the song of a single bird. Branches and leaves grew so thickly overhead that we might have been travelling in the dead of night. I thought of Tu Fu's poem:

> From scraps of cloud the wind blew down,
> Darkening the sun with dust.

Making our way through thickets of bamboo grass, fording streams and stumbling over rocks, with cold sweat running down our bodies all the while, we finally reached the Mogami district.

"Something untoward always happens on this route," said our guide with relief as he took his leave. "I was indeed fortunate to have brought you through safely."

Hearing that, even after it was all over, made our hearts pound.

🐑 Obanazawa, or "Pampas Vale"

At Obanazawa, we visited a man called Seifū. Although he was a rich man, he did not have a coarse manner or vulgar mind. He often went to Kyoto and he knew what it was like to travel. So he insisted we stay with him for several days to rest from our long journey, and he showed us all manner of hospitality.

> What a cool, summer breeze!
> Here, I make myself at home,
> Rest, and take my ease.

Come into the air!
　　Crawl from 'neath thy silkworm shed,
　　　Dear toad, croaking there.

A lady's eyebrow brush
　　Came to my mind when I saw
　　Safflowers in bloom.

How ancient the attire—
　　Unchanged for centuries—
　　　That silkworm keepers wear!
Sora

☽ The Hilltop Temple

In the domain of Yamagata is a hilltop temple called Ryūshaku-ji. Built in 860 by the great abbot Jikaku, it is situated in a particularly pure and tranquil spot. Many people told us we ought to see it, so we retraced our steps from Obanazawa, though the temple was about seventeen miles away.

It was still light, so after taking lodgings at a pilgrims' hostel at the foot of the hill, we climbed up to the temple on the hilltop. The hill consisted of massive boulders, one upon the other, out of which grew luxuriant pines and cypresses of great age, and the ancient earth and rocks were green with velvety moss.

The doors of all the lesser sanctuaries were closed and we heard not a single sound. But edging around the cliff and scrambling over the rocks, we finally said our prayers before the main Buddhist sanctum.

In the profound tranquillity and beauty of the place, our hearts felt deeply purified.

> In this hush profound,
>> Into the very rocks it seeps—
>>> The cicada sound.

🐚 Ōishida, or "Great Stonefield"

We wanted to go down the Mogami River in a boat, so we had to wait several days for fine weather at a place called Ōishida.

The seed of the old-fashioned *haikai* linked verse had once been sown here, and the people still practiced that style of verse, in love with it and unable to forget the days of its flowering. Their muse was as rustic as the sound of a reed pipe, and they trod the path of poetry with faltering step, hesitating at the crossroads, not knowing which way to take—the old or the new. They needed someone to guide them, so I left them a set of linked verse.

Who would have thought that on this, my own poetic pilgrimage, I would also be spreading abroad the Bashō style!

✿ The Mogami River

The Mogami River rises in the highlands of the far north. In its upper reaches here in Yamagata, there are some exceedingly dangerous rapids, such as "the Go Stones," where rocks are scattered about like black counters on a go board, and "the Peregrine Falcon," where the waters are as swift as a falcon's flight. Flowing north of Mount Itajiki, mentioned in an old poem, the Mogami finally empties into the sea at Sakata.

With mountains hanging over us on either side, we glided through thick foliage as we descended the river. Normally used for transporting rice, our craft was apparently called a "rice boat." Not far from where we could see the white threads of Shiraito Falls through spaces in the greenery stood Sennin-dō, "the Hall of the Mountain Wizard," poised on the edge of the waters.

The river was swollen with the rains and our journey was a perilous one.

> Gathering as it goes
> All the rains of June, how swiftly
> The Mogami flows!

✿ Haguro-yama

On the third day of the Sixth Moon [July 19], we

climbed to the retreat of the mountain ascetics on Haguro-yama (Featherblack Mountain). There we visited a follower of mine named Zushi Sakichi. He introduced us to the acting high priest, Ekaku the Acalya, who invited us to stay at a temple in Minami-dani (South Vale) and showed us great kindness, entertaining us most hospitably.

On the fourth, there was a poetry party at the main temple.

> When summer winds blow
> In this blest South Vale, they bring
> The cool fragrance of snow.

On the fifth day of the Sixth Moon [July 21], we visited Gongen Shrine, the first sanctuary to have been built on Mount Haguro. It is not known when Saint Nōjo, who founded it, lived, but the tenth-century *Engi Book of Ceremonies* mentions a shrine on U-shū-sato-yama, "Feather Province Hamlet Mountain." Perhaps someone made a mistake and wrote down 里 (hamlet) instead of 黒 (black).

And that makes me wonder if Haguro-yama was not perhaps originally "Feather Province Black Mountain," and the word "province" was accidentally left out, making it "Featherblack Mountain"! Apparently, this province came to be called Dewa (Payfeather) because in the official *Topographical Record* of the year 713, feathers are stipulated as its tribute. Haguro-yama, together with Gassan (Moon Mountain) and Yudono-yama (Bath Mountain), comprise the Dewa Sanzan, or "Three Holy Mountains of Dewa."

The temple on Mount Haguro is subject to Kan'ei-ji, a temple on Tōei Hill in Edo. It is of the Buddhist Tendai sect, whose doctrine of *shikan* (banish earthly thoughts and perceive Truth) is as clear and radiant as the full moon, and whose *endon yuzū* (perfection and harmony now, through unflagging obedience to Buddhist rules) shines like a light.

Cloisters stand row upon row, where mountain ascetics diligently practice these disciplines. The good emanating from this holy hill is most wonderful and awe-inspiring. It is a truly marvellous place and will surely prosper forever.

Gassan and Yudono-yama

On the eighth day of the Sixth Moon [July 24], we climbed Gassan, or "Moon Mountain." Wearing chain necklaces of mulberry paper to keep us free from impurity, and bleached cotton hoods, we were led by a so-called Strong Man, a mountain guide, as we climbed for nineteen miles through cloud and mist and over ice and snow until it seemed as if we too shared the very path of the sun and moon!

When we reached the summit, we were thoroughly chilled and could hardly breathe. The sun had already set and the moon had come out. Making ourselves a bed of bamboo grass with twigs of bamboo for a pillow, we lay down and waited for the dawn.

The sun finally rose, dispersing all the clouds, and we started down towards Yudono-yama.

As we neared the valley, we passed a hut that had once housed a forge. A Dewa Province swordsmith of the twelfth century chose this spot for its miraculous tempering waters. After cleansing both body and mind through abstinence, this craftsman made swords inscribed "Gassan" which came to be valued highly throughout the realm.

I thought of those swords tempered in China's Lung-chüan (Dragon Spring) and of Kanchiang and his wife Muyeh who forged fine blades together. I realized then that to excel in anything requires much more than ordinary effort.

As we sat down upon a rock to rest awhile, I noticed a small cherry tree nearby, no more than three feet tall and only half in bloom. To think this lovely late cherry, buried deep in snow all winter, did not forget to blossom when spring finally came to these mountains! Growing there fragrantly like the Zen koan, "Plum blossoms in the scorching sun," it reminded me of Gyōson's lines:

> Poor wild cherry tree!
> You've none but me to love you,
> And I've none, alas, but thee!

But the sight of these blossoms here on this mountain moved me even more deeply.

And now I lay down my writing brush, for what I saw on Yudono-yama I am forbidden by the rules for mountain pilgrims to reveal.

When we returned to our temple lodgings in South Vale, the Acalya asked for my poetic impressions of our pilgrimage to the Three Holy Mountains, and so I wrote the following for him on poem strips:

> How cool the crescent moon,
>   Faint above the leafy black
>   Of Mount Haguro!

> How many cloud shapes
>   Capped the peak before the moon
>   Rose on Moon Mountain?

> Since I may not tell
>   Of Yudono's wonders, tears
>   On my coat sleeve fall.

And Sora wrote:

> How they touch my heart:
>   Coins by faithful pilgrims strewn
>   On Yudono's path!

☁ Sakata

After leaving Mount Haguro, we went to the castle town of Tsuru-ga-Oka (Crane Hill) at the invitation of a samurai, Nagayama Ujishige, at whose home we composed a set of thirty-six stanzas of linked verse. My disciple Zushi Sakichi was there too, having come with us this far from Haguro-yama.

We then went by riverboat down to the port of Sakata, where we stayed at the home of the physician En'an Fugyoku.

> From far Hot Spring Hills
> All the way to Windy Beach—
> How cool the evening view!

> The river Mogami
> Has drowned the hot, summer sun
> And sunk it in the sea!

☆ Kisakata

Countless are the beauties of land and sea that I have already seen, but now my heart quickened at the prospect of seeing Kisakata, the celebrated lagoon about twenty-four miles northeast of Sakata Harbor. We made our way over hills and along beaches, trudging through sand dunes, and we reached our destination just as the sun was setting.

A wind had blown up from the sea, filling the air with sand and driving rain, and we could not even see Mount Chōkai. There was a curious fascination about groping our way in the dark merely imagining the beauties that lay before us, and the rain gave promise of an even finer view than usual on clearing. We squeezed into a fisherman's shed roofed over with rushes and waited there for the rain to cease.

Next morning the sky was cloudless, and when the sun had risen and was shining brilliantly, we went out upon the lagoon in a boat.

After visiting Nōin's Isle to see where the poet-priest Nōin had spent his three-year retreat, we landed on the shore of an island just beyond. There we found an ancient cherry tree. It was the very one whose reflections in the water Saigyō referred to when he wrote:

> Sculling over cherry blossoms,
> Go the fishermen in boats.

The tree was a living monument to the poet.

On the edge of the lagoon was an imperial tomb said to be the burial place of the Empress Jingū [regent, 201–269]. The temple there was called Kanmanju-ji. I had not heard that the empress had visited this place. I wondered why she was buried here.

We sat down in the abbot's chambers of the temple, and when the finely woven bamboo-and-brocade curtains were rolled up, the whole panorama of Kisa Lagoon lay before us.

To the south, Mount Chōkai looked as if it were propping up the heavens and its image was reflected in the lagoon. Westward the road was barred by the Uyamuya Barrier, but to the east an embankment carried the road off into the far distance towards Akita. The sea lay to the north, and the place where it entered the lagoon was called Shiogoshi, or "Tideway."

Though the lagoon called Kisakata was little more than two miles long and two miles wide, it reminded me of Matsushima. But in some ways it was quite different. While Matsushima had a gay, laughing beauty, Kisakata's face was full of bitterness and rue. There was a sense of the desolate loneliness and sorrow of a tormented soul.

> In Kisakata's rain,
> > Mimosas droop, like fair Hsi-shih
> > Who languished with love's pain.

> Cool seascape with cranes
> > Wading long-legged in the pools
> > Mid the Tideway dunes.

On the occasion of the Shiogoshi Festival:

> I wonder what they eat
> At Shiogoshi's Festival.
> > What's their special treat?
> > > *Sora*

[Moved by the sight of a poor family who had laid a wooden shutter on the ground to sit upon—their humble dwelling having no veranda:]

> How humbly fishers dwell,
>> With but a board laid on the sand
>>> To savor evening's cool.
>>>> *Teiji*. A merchant
>>>> from Mino Province

On seeing a pair of ospreys nesting on a rock near the sea:

> With your nest on a rock,
>> Have you a truce with the ocean waves,
>>> O trusting sea hawk?
>>>> *Sora*

🐑 The North Road

We lingered for days at Sakata, until the clouds above the North Road began to beckon. But our hearts failed us at the thought of the great distance ahead when we heard it was three hundred miles to the capital of Kaga Province.

After passing the Nezu Barrier into the province of Echigo, we set off again with fresh resolve and eventually reached Ichiburi Barrier in Etchū Province. We had been nine days on the road. In the oppressive heat and rain, I was plagued by my old complaint—but I shall not write about that.

> It's Tanabata Eve!
>   Tomorrow Cowherd meets his Weaver:
>   The lover-stars' reprieve!

> O'er wild ocean spray,
>   All the way to Sado Isle
>   Spreads the Milky Way!

Today, we passed the most perilous places in all the North. The precarious path led us over boulders at the foot of a sheer cliff against which huge waves break. It was every man for himself, as the names of the worst spots implied: "Oblivious of Parent, Oblivious of Child," "Dogs Turn Back," and "Send Back Your Horse."

We were exhausted and went to bed early, but in a nearby room I heard voices I judged to be those of two young women. The voice of an old man mingled with theirs. I gathered they were ladies of pleasure from the port town of Niigata, in Echigo, on a long pilgrimage to the Grand Shrine at Ise. The man had come with them as far as this barrier, and they were writing letters for him to take back to Niigata the next day and giving him sentimental messages to deliver. As I listened, I wove into their whispers an echo of a poem by a courtesan of long ago.

Where the white waves foam
  As they break upon the shore,
  We are sea wrack evermore,
Like fisherfolk without a home.
Making fickle love each night
  Is our karma and our fate.
  To have fallen to this state:
What a sorry, sorry plight!

I fell asleep listening to their chatter, and the next morning, as we were about to set off, one of the young women approached us.

"We do not know the way," she said. "We are helpless and afraid. May we follow you at a discreet distance?" There were tears in her eyes as she went on. "Extend to us, we beg you, your priestly mercy and compassion so we too may feel the blessing of the Buddha."

"I fear we stop too often along the road," I replied. "But there will be others to follow, who are going your way. May God protect you." For a long time after we left them, my heart overflowed with pity, and I could not get them out of my mind.

'Neath the selfsame roof
  I slept with a courtesan! like moon
    With bush clover, forsooth.

I told Sora my poem and he wrote it down.

☽ Nago-no-Ura

We forded "the Forty-Eight Streams" at the delta of the Kurobe River and countless other streams and rivers too. Finally we came to Nago Beach.

The *Manyōshū* poet's "Waving wistarias" of Tako were not far from there. Although it was no longer spring, we thought it might be worth seeing how the vines looked in early autumn, so we asked someone how to get there.

" 'Tis about twelve miles along the beach from here," the man said, "in the lee of yonder hill. But there be but few houses there, and only fishermen's shacks at that. You'll find no one to give you a night's lodging."

He discouraged us so much that we went straight on to Kaga Province.

> Through fragrant fields
> Of early rice we went, beside
> The wild Ariso Sea.

☙ Kanazawa

After crossing Snowflower Hill and Kurikara Vale, we arrived in the great castle town of Kanazawa on the fifteenth day of the Seventh Moon [August 30]. Kasho, a merchant we knew who often came to Kanazawa from Osaka, happened to be here, so we joined him at his inn.

Isshō, a young poet of considerable local renown with a great love for linked verse, had died the winter before, and his elder brother was holding a memorial service for him. Isshō was a disciple of mine and we had both looked forward to viewing the autumn moon together. At his grave, I wrote:

> The autumn wind's sigh
> Is my heart's sorrowing cry.
> Oh, shake the mound! Reply!

We were invited to a certain person's hermitage:

> How cool the autumn air!
> I'll peel them and enjoy them—
> The melon and the pear.

A poem composed on the way:

> How hot the sun glows,
> Pretending not to notice
> An autumn wind blows!

And at a place called Komatsu, or "Little Pines":

> The autumn wind blows through
> Little Pines—a lovely name—
> Bush clover and pampas too.

☆ Tada Shrine

At Komatsu, we visited Tada Shrine. There we saw the helmet of the warrior Sanemori [1111–1183] and a piece of his brocade armor robe. They are said to have been given him by Lord Yoshitomo of Minamoto, when Sanemori served with the Genji clan.

It was no ordinary helmet. From its peak to the turned-back ear flanges, it was embellished all over with chrysanthemum arabesques in gold. The crest was a dragon's head, and the helmet had flat, gilded "horns" that were proud and graceful.

When Sanemori was killed in battle, Kiso Yoshinaka sent Jirō of Higuchi to offer these relics to the shrine. All this is vividly recorded in the shrine's chronicles.

> What a tragic thing:
>   'Neath a mighty warrior's helm
>   Grasshoppers chirruping!

🐑 Nata-dera

On the road to Yamanaka Hot Springs, we could see Shirane-ga-Take, "White Mountain," which stayed behind us all the way. In the foothills to our left was a temple dedicated to Kannon, the Goddess of Mercy. After Emperor Kazan [968–1008] had made a pilgrimage to the Thirty-Three Holy Places in the western provinces, he is said to have enshrined here an image of the Most Merciful Kannon, the Bodhisattva of Great Love and Compassion. He called this temple Nata, combining the first syllables of Nachi and Tanigumi, the first and last of the Thirty-Three Holy Places.

Amidst an assortment of curiously shaped rocks and old gnarled pines was a small sanctuary with thatched roof, built atop a rock. The age-whitened purity of these boulders gave this place a mournful beauty exceeding that of the famed Ishiyama Temple at Ōmi.

> Ishiyama stone
> Is not so white, and whiter still
> Is autumn, windblown!

☽ Yamanaka Spa

We bathed in the waters of Yamanaka's hot springs. In curative powers they are second only, people say, to the hot springs at Ariake.

> Yamanaka's waters be
> Better than chrysanthemums
> For longevity!

The proprietor of our inn, still a youth, was called Kumenosuke. His father is said to have been very fond of poetry, and the story is told here of how a young, aspiring poet from Kyoto was so humiliated by the innkeeper's superior poetic ability that when he returned to Kyoto he took lessons in composition from Teitoku, and went on to become the celebrated poet we know as Teishitsu. When famous and much sought after, Teishitsu would never accept payment, people say, from these villagers for criticism or correction of their poetry.

Sora was taken ill. Since he had relatives in a place called Nagashima in Ise Province, we decided he should go on ahead.

> A solitary rover,
> If I fall, then let me die
> Amid bush clover.

Sora wrote this poem before he left.

With the sadness of the one who goes and the grief of the one who is left behind, we were like a pair of wild ducks parted from each other and lost in the clouds. I wrote:

> Tears of autumn dew
> Will wash off my hat the words
> "Travellers two."

🐒 Zenshō-ji

I spent the night at a temple called Zenshō-ji on the outskirts of the town of Daishōji. I was still in the province of Kaga. Sora had stayed at the temple the night before and had left a poem:

> All through the night
>   I listened to the autumn wind
>   In the lonely hills.

We were only one night apart, but it seemed like a thousand miles. I, too, listened to the autumn wind as I lay awake. As dawn approached, I could hear the priests chanting. Then a gong sounded and we all went in to the refectory.

Since I wanted to reach Echizen Province that same day, I started to leave in a great hurry, but a young monk came running down the steps after me with some paper and an ink stone. Just then, some leaves from a willow tree in the garden fluttered to the ground.

> Your kindness to repay,
>   Would I might sweep the fallen
>   Willow leaves away!

My straw sandals were already tied on, so I did not even take the time to read over my hurried lines.

☆ The Road to Eihei-ji

Crossing by boat the narrow mouth of Yoshizaki Inlet on the border of Echizen Province, we stopped to see the celebrated Pines of Shiogoshi.

> All the wild night through,
>   Battered by the great typhoon
>   Waves and winds that blew,
> In their limbs they held the moon—
> The pines on Shiogoshi dune.

Saigyō

So many poems had been written there, nothing new was left to say about the many lovely views. To write another word about Shiogoshi's pines would have been like trying to add a sixth finger to the hand.

The chief priest of Tenryū-ji in the town of Maruoka was someone I had known for a long time, so I went to see him. Then there was Hokushi, who had come with us from Kanazawa. He had intended to come only part of the way to see us off, but finally he followed me all the way to Maruoka. He did not miss a single beauty spot and kept composing poems all the way. Some of his ideas were quite profound. I wrote him a parting poem:

> I'll scribble something on it
>   And tear up my faithful summer fan:
>   Just a farewell sonnet!

Walking about three and a half miles towards the

hills, I visited Eihei-ji. This temple was founded by the Zen priest Dōgen [1200–1253]. I believe he had some noble reason for establishing his temple so deep in the hills and well outside the "Thousand Li Radius" of the capital, Kyoto.

Fukui and Tsuruga

Although it was only seven miles to the castle town of Fukui, I did not set out until after I had eaten my evening meal, and my steps faltered as I made my way along the road in the dusk.

There was a man in Fukui named Tōsai who had lived there as a recluse for a long time. He had visited me once in Edo, but that was more than ten years ago, so he must be very old by now, I thought—or perhaps dead. However, when I asked some people about him, they said he was still living and told me where he dwelt.

In a quiet lane, away from the bustle of the town, I found a small and humble cottage overgrown with vines of moonflower and loofah, its door completely hidden by cockscomb and broom cypress. This must be it, I thought, and knocked at the gate. A woman came out who looked quite poor. "From whence come you, Holy Father?" she inquired, then continued: "My master is at a friend's house nearby. If you wish to see him, you will find him there." I assumed she was his wife. It was rather like a scene from *The Tale of Genji*, I thought, as I went to find him.

I spent two nights at Tōsai's house, and then said I must go, for I wanted to see the harvest moon at Tsuruga Harbor. Tōsai insisted on accompanying me, and tucking up his kimono and stuffing the ends into his sash, he set off in high spirits as my guide.

Gradually, Shirane-ga-Take, "White Mountain," disappeared from view and Mount Hino came into sight. We crossed the Bridge of Asamuzu, oft-mentioned in poems, where the "reeds of Tamae" were already in flower. Passing Bush Warbler Barrier and crossing Hot Spring Ridge Pass, we heard the call of the first wild geese at Hiuchi-ga-Jo (Flint Castle) and then at Kaeru-yama (the Hill Where They Return), and on the evening of the fourteenth day of the Eighth Moon [September 28], we arrived at the harbor town of Tsuruga and found an inn.

That night, the moonlit sky was uncommonly clear. "Will it be fine again tomorrow night?" I asked, but the innkeeper replied, "Here in the North it is never possible to say with any certainty whether it will be fine or cloudy on the morrow." We drank wine with him and afterwards paid a night visit to Myōjin Shrine at a place called Kehi where Emperor Chūai [r. 192–200] was enshrined.

There was a holy atmosphere about the place, and in the moonlight that filtered through the pine trees, the white sand before the shrine looked like frost. "In ancient times," said our host, "the successor to the founder of this sect, the Second Chief High Priest, in his desire to save souls, himself cleared away the grass, carried earth and stone, and dried up the surrounding marsh, so that worshippers could forever after come and go with ease. In commemoration of his deed, it is the custom, even to this day, for the Chief High Priest of the Shinto Jishū sect to bring sand to spread before the shrine. The ceremony is called the High Priest's Sand Bringing."

> How holy, pure, and white,
> > The sand brought by the Chief High Priest
> > Shines in the moonlight!

On the fifteenth, the night of the full moon, just as the innkeeper said it might, it rained.

> > Ah me! what a time
> > > To rain—the night of Harvest Moon.
> > > Oh, fickle northern clime!

☽ Iro-no-Hama

On the sixteenth day of the Eighth Moon [September 30], the weather was fine, and I wanted to collect some of the tiny pink *donacilla* shells, so we took a boat to Pink

Beach. It was seventeen miles across the water, but a kind gentleman by the name of Tenya had thoughtfully filled our boat with picnic boxes and bamboos of saké and had provided several of his servants to assist us. A favorable wind got us there in no time.

There were a few fishermen's huts on the shore and a shabby-looking temple of the Buddhist Hokke sect. There, we drank tea and heated our saké, and savored the melancholy beauty of the evening scene.

> Sadder and much more
> Forlorn even than at Suma
> Is autumn on this shore.

> Each wave turning over
> Leaves a trail of tiny shells
> And petals of bush clover.

I asked Tōsai to write a short account of our day's outing, and we left it at the temple.

Ōgaki

Rotsū, one of my disciples, came to Tsuruga to meet me, and we travelled together to Mino Province. We arrived at the castle town of Ōgaki on horseback, and Sora joined us there, having come from Ise. Etsujin had galloped there too on his horse, and we all gathered at the retired samurai Jokō's house.

Viscount Zensen, samurai Keikō and his sons, and other dear friends kept arriving by day and night, greeting me with both joy and concern, as if I had come back from the dead.

And now, though I have not yet recovered fully from the fatigue of my journey, it is already the sixth day of the Ninth Moon [October 18], and I wish to go to Ise Shrine to see the ceremony that takes place only once every twenty-one years, when the Deity is transferred to a newly built shrine. It is already late autumn, so I shall set off once more, in a boat, for Futami-ga-Ura shore where the clams are so delicious, but now, alas,

> Sadly, I part from you;
> > Like a clam torn from its shell,
> > > I go, and autumn too.

☆ Epilogue

[Written by Soryū, a scholar-priest who prepared the final draft for the original edition.]

In this slim volume, you will find prose of spare simplicity, and phrases of beautifully polished elegance. You will find writing of robust, masculine strength, as well as touches of delicate, feminine grace.

As you read *The Narrow Road to a Far Province*, at times you will find yourself rising up to applaud. At other times you will quietly hang your head with emotion.

Perhaps you will want to put on your straw rain cape and set off upon a similar journey, or you may be content to sit still and imagine the enchanting views as they pass before your mind's eye—so multifarious are the impressions limned herein in prose as beautiful as mermaids' tears.

What a fascinating journey! What writing skill! How sad that a man of such talent is now so frail, with the hoarfrost ever increasing upon his brows!

> *Soryū*
> Early summer of the Seventh
> Year of Genroku [1694]

奥 の 細 道

序章

月日は百代の過客にして，行きかふ年も又旅人なり舟の上に生涯をうかべ馬の口とらへて老をむかふる者は，日々旅にして旅を栖とす．古人も多く旅に死せるあり．予もいづれの年よりか，片雲の風にさそはれて漂泊の思ひやまず，海浜にさすらへ，去年の秋江上の破屋に蜘の古巣をはらひて，やや年も暮れ春立てる霞の空に，白河の関越えんとそぞろ神のものにつきて心をくるはせ，道祖神のまねきにあひて取るもの手につかず，股引の破れをつづり，笠の緒付けかへて，三里に灸すうるより，松島の月まづ心にかかりて，住める方は人に譲り杉風が別墅に移るに，

　　草の戸も住替る代ぞ雛の家

表八句を庵の柱に懸け置く。

旅立

弥生も末の七日，あけぼのの空朧々として，月は有明にて光をさまれるものから，富士の峰幽かに見えて，上野・谷中の花の梢又いつかはと心ぼそし．むつまじきかぎりは宵よりつどひて，舟に

乗りて送る．千住といふ所にて船をあがれば，前途三千里のおもひ胸にふさがりて，幻のちまたに離別の泪をそそぐ．

　　行く春や鳥啼き魚の目は泪

これを矢立の初めとして行く道なほ進まず．人々は途中に立ちならびて，後かげの見ゆるまではと見送るなるべし．

　　✿　　草加

ことし元禄二年にや，奥羽長途の行脚ただかりそめに思ひたちて，呉天に白髪の恨を重ぬといへども，耳にふれていまだ目に見ぬ境，もし生きて帰らばと定めなき頼の末をかけ，その日漸草加といふ宿にたどり着きにけり．痩骨の肩にかかれる物，まづ苦しむ．ただ身すがらにと出立ち侍るを，紙子一衣は夜の防ぎ，浴衣・雨具・墨筆のたぐひ，あるはさりがたき餞などしたるは，さすがにうち捨てがたくて，路次の煩となれるこそわりなけれ．

室の八島に詣す．同行曽良が曰く，「この神は木の花さくや姫の神と申して富士一躰なり．無戸室に入りて焼き給ふ誓のみ中に火々出見の尊生れ給ひしより，室の八島と申す．又，煙を詠み習し侍るも，この謂なり」．はた，このしろといふ魚を禁ず，縁起の旨，

90

世に伝ふ事も侍りし.

仏五左衛門

三十日, 日光山の麓に泊る. あるじの言ひける やう, 「我が名を仏五左衛門と言ふ. 万正直を旨とするゆゑに人かくは申し侍るまま, 一夜の草の枕もうちとけて休み給へ」と言ふ. いかなる仏の濁世塵土に示現して, かかる桑門の乞食順礼ごときの人をたすけ給ふにやと, あるじのなす事に心をとどめてみるに, ただ無智無分別にして正直偏固の者なり. 剛毅木訥の仁に近きたぐひ, 気稟の清質, もつとも尊ぶべし.

日光

卯月朔日, 御山に詣拝す. 往昔, の御山を「二荒山」と書きしを, 空海大師開基の時, 「日光」と改め給ふ. 千歳未来を悟り給ふにや, 今この御光一天にかかやきて, 恩沢八荒にあふれ, 四民安堵の栖穏やかなり. なほ憚り多くて筆をさし置きぬ.

あらたふと青葉若葉の日の光

91

黒髪山は霞かかりて，雪いまだ白し．

　　剃捨てて黒髪山に衣更　　　　　　　　　　　　　曽良

曽良は河合氏にして，惣五郎といへり．芭蕉の下葉に軒を並べて，
予が薪水の労を助く．このたび松島・象潟の眺めともにせん事を
悦び，且つは羇旅の難をいたはらんと，旅立つ暁髪を剃りて墨
染にさまをかへ，惣五を改めて宗悟とす．よつて黒髪山の句あ
り．「衣更」の二字，力ありてきこゆ．
二十余丁山を登つて滝あり．岩洞の頂より飛流して百尺，千岩
の碧潭に落ちたり．岩窟に身をひそめ入りて滝の裏より見れば，
裏見の滝と申し伝へ侍るなり．

　　暫時は滝に籠るや夏の初め

那須の黒羽といふ所に知人あれば，これより野越にかかりて直道
を行かんとす．遙かに一村を見かけて行くに，雨降り日暮るる．
農夫の家に一夜を借りて，明くれば又野中を行く．そこに野飼の
馬あり．草苅る男に嘆きよれば，野夫といへどもさすがに情しら
ぬにはあらず，「いかがすべきや，されども，この野は縦横にわ
かれて，うひうひしき旅人の道ふみたがへん，あやしう侍れば，
この馬のとどまる所にて馬を返し給へ」と貸し侍りぬ．小さき者
ふたり，馬の跡したひて走る．一人は小姫にて名を「かさね」と
言ふ．聞きなれぬ名のやさしかりければ，

かさねとは八重撫子の名なるべし　　　曽良

やがて人里に至れば，価を鞍壺に結び付けて馬を返しぬ.

黒羽

黒羽の館代浄坊寺何某の方におとづる．思ひがけぬあるじの悦び，日夜語りつづけて，その弟桃翠などいふが朝夕勤めとぶらひ，自らの家にも伴ひて，親属の方にも招かれ日をふるままに，一日郊外に逍遥して犬追物の跡を一見し，那須の篠原を分けて玉藻の前の古墳をとふ．それより八幡宮に詣づ．与市扇の的を射し時，「別しては我が国氏神正八幡」と誓ひしも，この神社にて侍ると聞けば，感応殊にしきりに覚えらる．暮るれば桃翠宅に帰る.
修験光明寺といふあり．そこに招かれて行者堂を拝す.

　　夏山に足駄を拝む首途かな

93

☆　雲岩寺

当国雲岩寺の奥に仏頂和尚山居の跡あり.

　「竪横の五尺にたらぬ草の庵

　　　むすぶもくやし雨なかりせば

と松の炭して岩に書付け侍り」と，いつぞや聞え給ふ. その跡見んと雲岩寺に杖を曳けば，人々進んでともにいざなひ，若き人おほく道のほどうち騒ぎて，おぼえずかの麓に到る. 山は奥あるけしきにて. 谷道遙かに松杉黒く苔しただりて，卯月の天今なほ寒し. 十景尽くる所. 橋を渡つて山門に入る，さて，かの跡はいづくのほどにやと，後の山によぢのぼれば，石上の小庵岩窟にむすびかけたり. 妙禅師の死関・法雲法師の石室を見るがごとし.

　　木啄も庵はやぶらず夏木立

と，とりあへぬ一句を柱に残し侍りし.

94

殺生石

これより殺生石に行く. 館代より馬にて送らる. この口付の男,
「短冊得させよ」と乞ふ. やさしき事を望み侍るものかなと,

　　野を横に馬牽きむけよほととぎす

殺生石は温泉の出る山陰にあり. 石の毒気いまだほろびず, 蜂・
蝶のたぐひ真砂の色の見えぬほどかさなり死す.

芦野の西行柳

又, 清水ながるるの柳は芦野の里にありて田の畔に残る. この所
の郡守戸部某の「この柳見せばやな」と折々にのたまひ聞え給
ふを, いづくのほどにやと思ひしを, 今日この柳のかげにこそ立
ちより侍りつれ.

　　田一枚植ゑて立去る柳かな

白河の関

心もとなき日かず重るままに，白河の関にかかりて旅心定りぬ．「いかで都へ」と便求めしも 断 なり．中にもこの関は三関の一にして，風騒の人心をとどむ．秋風を耳に残し，紅葉を 俤 にして，青葉の梢なほあはれなり．卯の花の白妙に，茨の花の咲きそひて，雪にも越ゆる心地ぞする．古人 冠 を正し衣装を改めし事など，清輔の筆にもとどめ置かれしとぞ．

　　卯の花をかざしに関の晴着かな　　　　　曽良

須賀川

とかくして越え行くままに，阿武隈川を渡る．左に会津根高く，右に岩城・相馬・三春の庄，常陸・下野の地をさかひて山つらなる．かげ沼といふ所を行くに，今日は空曇りて物影うつらず．須賀川の駅に等窮といふものを尋ねて，四五日とどめらる．まづ「白河の関いかに越えつるや」と問ふ．「長途の苦しみ身心つかれ，且つは風景に魂うばはれ，懐旧に 腸 を断ちて，はかばかしう思ひめぐらさず．

風流の初めや奥の田植うた

無下に越えんもさすがに」と語れば，脇・第三とつづけて三巻と
なしぬ．
　この宿の傍に，大きなる栗の木陰をたのみて，世をいとふ僧あ
り．橡ひろふ太山もかくやと閑に覚えられて，ものに書付け侍
る．その詞，

> 栗といふ文字は西の木と書きて，
> 西方浄土に便ありと，行基菩薩の
> 一生杖にも柱にもこの木を用ひ給
> ふとかや，

　世 の 人 の 見 付 け ぬ 花 や 軒 の 栗

　🐑　**安積沼**

等窮が宅を出でて五里ばかり，檜皮の宿を離れて安積山あり．路
より近く．このあたり沼多し．かつみ刈る比もやや近うなれば，
いづれの草を花かつみとはいふぞと，人々に尋ね侍れども，更に
知る人なし．沼を尋ね，人に問ひ，「かつみかつみ」と尋ねありき
て，日は山の端にかかりぬ．二本松より右にきれて，黒塚の岩屋
一見し，福島に宿る．

🌙 信夫もぢ摺の石

明くれば，しのぶもぢ摺の石を尋ねて，信夫の里に行く．遥か山陰の小里に，石半ば上に埋れてあり．里の童の来りて教へける，「昔はこの山の上に侍りしを，往来の人の麦草をあらして この石を試み侍るをにくみて，この谷につき落せば，石の面下ざまに伏したり」と言ふ．さもあるべき事にや．

早苗とる手もとや昔しのぶ摺

☁ 佐藤庄司の旧跡

月の輪の渡しを越えて，瀬の上といふ宿に出づ．佐藤庄司が旧跡は左の山際一里半ばかりにあり．飯塚の里鯖野と聞きて尋ね尋ね行くに，丸山といふに尋ねあたる．これ，庄司が旧館なり．麓に大手の跡など人の教ふるにまかせて泪を落し，又かたはらの古寺に一家の石碑を残す．中にも二人の嫁がしるし，まづ哀れなり．女なれどもかひがひしき名の世に聞えつるものかなと袂をぬらしぬ．堕涙の石碑も遠きにあらず．寺に入りて茶を乞へば，ここに義経の太刀・弁慶が笈をとどめて什物とす．

98

笈も太刀も五月にかざれ紙幟

五月朔日の事なり.

☆　飯塚

その夜，飯塚にとまる．温泉あれば湯に入りて宿を借るに，土坐に筵を敷きて，あやしき貧家なり．灯もなければ，ゐろりの火かげに寝所を設けて臥す．夜に入りて，雷鳴り雨しきりに降りて，臥せる上よりもり，蚤・蚊にせせられて眠らず，持病さへおこりて消入るばかりになん．短夜の空もやうやう明くれば，又旅立ちぬ．なほ夜のなごり，心進まず，馬借りて桑折の駅に出づる．遙かなる行末をかかへて，かかる病おぼつかなしといへど，羈旅辺土の行脚，捨身無常の観念，道路に死なん，これ天の命なりと，気力聊かとり直し，路縦横に踏んで伊達の大木戸を越す．

🐑　笠島

鐙摺・白石の城を過ぎ，笠島の郡に入れば，藤中将実方の塚はいづくのほどならんと人に問へば，「これより遙か右に見ゆる山際

99

の里を蓑輪・笠島といひ，道祖神の社・かたみの薄今にあり」と教ふ．この比の五月雨に道いとあしく，身疲れ侍れば，よそながら眺めやりて過ぐるに，蓑輪・笠島も五月雨の折にふれたりと，

　　笠島はいづこ五月のぬかり道

　　🌙　武隈の松

岩沼に宿る．

武隈の松にこそ目覚むる心地はすれ．根は土際より二木に分れて，昔の姿うしなはずと知らる．まづ，能因法師思ひ出づ．往昔，陸奥守にて下りし人，この木を伐りて名取川の橋杭にせられたる事などあればにや，「松はこのたび跡もなし」とは詠みたり．代々，あるは伐り，あるいは植継ぎなどせしと聞くに，今はた千歳の形ととのほひて，めでたき松のけしきになん侍りし．

　　「武隈の松みせ申せ遅桜」と挙白
　　といふ者の餞別したりければ，

　　桜より松は二木を三月越し

🌸 仙台

名取川を渡りて仙台に入る．あやめ葺く日なり．旅宿をもとめて四五日逗留す．ここに画工加右衛門といふものあり．聊か心ある者と聞きて，知人になる．この者，年比さだかならぬ名所を考へ置き侍ればとて，一日案内．宮城野の萩茂りあひて秋の気色思ひやらるる．玉田・横野，つつじが岡はあせび咲くころなり．日影ももらぬ松の林に入りて，ここを木の下といふとぞ．昔もかく露ふかければこそ「みさぶらひみかさ」とは詠みたれ．薬師堂・天神の御社など拝みて，その日は暮れぬ．なほ松島・塩釜の所々画に書きて贈る．且つ，紺の染緒つけたる草鞋二足餞す．さればこそ風流のしれ者，ここに至りてその実を顕はす．

あやめ草足に結ばん草鞋の緒

⭐ 壺の碑

かの画図にまかせてたどり行けば，おくの細道の山際に十付の菅あり．今も年々十符の菅菰を調へて国守に献ずといへり．

　壺碑　　市川村多賀城にあり．

つぼの石ぶみは，高さ六尺余，横三尺ばかりか．苔を穿ちて文字

幽かなり。四維国界の数里を記す。「此城、神亀元年、按察使鎮守府将軍大野朝臣東人之所里也。天平宝字六年、参議東海東山節度使同将軍恵美朝臣獶修造而。十二月朔日」とあり。聖武皇帝の御時に当れり。昔より詠み置ける歌枕、多く語り伝ふといへども、山崩れ川流れて道あらたまり、石は埋れて土にかくれ、木は老いて若木にかはれば、時移り代変じてその跡たしかならぬ事のみを、ここに至りて疑ひなき千歳の記念、今眼前に古人の心を閲す。行脚の一徳、存命の悦び、羇旅の労を忘れて泪も落つるばかりなり。

末の松山

それより野田の玉川・沖の石を尋ぬ。末の松山は寺を造りて末松山といふ。松のあひあひ皆墓はらにて、翼をかはし枝をつらぬる契の末も、終にはかくのごときと悲しさも増りて、塩釜の浦に入相の鐘を聞く。五月雨の空聊か晴れて、夕月夜幽かに、籬が島もほど近し。蜑の小舟こぎつれて肴わかつ声々に、「つなでかなしも」と詠みけん心も知られて、いとど哀れなり。その夜、目盲法師の琵琶をならして奥浄瑠璃といふものを語る、平家にもあらず舞にもあらず。ひなびたる調子うち上げて枕近うかしましけれど、さすがに辺土の遺風忘れざるものから殊勝に覚えらる。

🌙 塩釜

早朝，塩釜の明神に詣づ．国守再興せられて，宮柱ふとしく彩椽きらびやかに，石の階 九仞に重り，朝日朱の玉垣をかかやかす．かかる道の果，塵土の境まで，神霊あらたにましますこそ吾国の風俗なれと，いと貴けれ．神前に古き宝燈あり．鉄の戸びらの面に「文治三年和泉三郎寄進」とあり．五百年来の俤，今目の前にうかびて，そぞろに珍し．かれは勇義忠孝の士なり．佳名今に至りて，慕はずといふ事なし．誠に，人よく道を勤め義を守るべし．「名もまたこれにしたがふ」と言へり．

☁️ 松島

日既に午にちかし．船をかりて松島にわたる．その間二里余，雄島の磯につく．抑，ことふりにたれど，松島は扶桑第一の好風にして，およそ洞庭・西湖を恥ぢず．東南より海を入れて江の中三里，浙江の潮をたたふ．島々の数を尽して，欹つものは天を指し，伏すものは波に匍匐ふ．あるは二重にかさなり三重に畳みて，左にわかれ右につらなる．負へるあり抱けるあり，児孫愛すがごとし．松の緑こまやかに，枝葉汐風に吹きたわめて，屈曲おのづから矯めたるがごとし．その気色窅然として美人の顔を

103

粧ふ. ちはやぶる神の昔, 大山祇のなせるわざにや. 造化の天工,
いづれの人か筆をふるひ詞を尽さむ.

雄島が磯は地つづきて海に出でたる島なり. 雲居禅師の別室の
跡, 坐禅石などあり. はた, 松の木陰に世をいとふ人も稀々見え
侍りて, 落穂・松笠などうち煙りたる草の庵閑に住みなし, い
かなる人とは知られずながら, まづなつかしく立ち寄るほどに,
月海にうつりて昼のながめ又あらたむ. 江上に帰りて宿を求むれ
ば, 窓をひらき二階を作りて, 風雲の中に旅寝するこそ, あやし
きまで妙なる心地はせらるれ.

　　　松 島 や 鶴 に 身 を 借 れ ほ と と ぎ す　　　　　　曽良

予は口を閉ぢて眠らんとして寝ねらず. 旧庵をわかるる時, 素堂
松島の詩あり, 原安適松が浦島の和歌を贈らる. 袋を解きて, こ
よひの友とす. 且つ杉風・濁子が発句あり.

☆　瑞巌寺

十一日, 瑞巌寺に詣づ. 当寺三十二世の昔, 真壁の平四郎出家し
て入唐, 帰朝の後開山す. その後に雲居禅師の徳化によりて, 七
堂甍改まりて, 金碧荘厳光を輝かし, 仏土成就の大伽藍とはな
れりける. かの見仏聖の寺はいづくにやとしたはる.

104

🐑 石巻

十二日，平泉と志し，あねはの松・緒だえの橋など聞き伝へて，人跡稀に雉兎蒭蕘の往きかふ道，そことも分かず，終に路ふみたがへて石の巻といふ湊に出づ．

「こがね花咲く」と詠みて奉りたる金華山海上に見わたし，数百の廻船入江につどひ，人家地をあらそひて，竈の煙立ちつづけたり．思ひがけずかかる所にも来れるかなと，宿からんとすれど更に宿かす人なし．漸まどしき小家に一夜をあかして，明くれば又しらぬ道まよひ行く．袖の渡り・尾ぶちの牧・真野の萱原など，よそ目に見て，遙かなる堤を行く，心細き長沼にそうて，戸伊摩といふ所に一宿して平泉に到る．その間二十余里ほどとおぼゆ．

🌙 平泉

三代の栄耀一睡の中にして，大門の跡は一里こなたにあり．秀衡が跡は田野になりて，金鶏山のみ形を残す．まづ高館にのぼれば，北上川南部より流るる大河なり．衣川は和泉が城をめぐりて，高館の下にて大河に落ち入る．泰衡等が旧跡は，衣が関を隔てて南部口をさし堅め，夷をふせぐとみえたり．さても義臣すぐ

つてこの城にこもり，功名一時の 叢 となる．「国破れて山河あ
り，城春にして草青みたり」と，笠うち敷きて時のうつるまで泪
を落し侍りぬ．

　　　夏草や兵どもが夢の跡

　　　卯の花に兼房みゆる白毛かな　　　　　　　　　曽良

かねて耳驚かしたる二堂開帳す．経堂は三将の像を残し，光堂は
三代の棺を納め，三尊の仏を安置す．七宝散りうせて珠の扉風に
やぶれ，金の柱霜雪に朽ちて既に頽廃空虚の 叢 となるべきを，
四面新に囲みて，甍を覆ひて風雨を凌ぐ．暫時，千歳の記念とは
なれり．

　　　五月雨の降りのこしてや光堂

　　　🐌　尿前の関

南部道遙かに見やりて，岩手の里に泊る．小黒崎・美豆の小島を
過ぎて，鳴子の湯より尿前の関にかかりて，出羽の国に越えんと
す．この路旅人稀なる所なれば，関守にあやしめられて，漸 と
して関を越す．大山をのぼつて日既に暮れければ，封人の家を見

かけて舎を求む．三日風雨あれて，よしなき山中に逗留す．

蚤虱馬の尿する枕もと

☆ 尿前の関

あるじの言ふ，これより出羽の国に大山を隔てて，道さだかなら
ざれば，道しるべの人を頼みて越ゆべきよしを申す．さらばと言
ひて，人を頼み侍れば，究竟の若者反脇指をよこたへ，樫の杖を
携へて，我々が先に立ちて行く．今日こそ必ずあやふきめにもあ
ふべき日なれと，辛き思ひをなして後について行く．あるじの言
ふにたがはず，高山森々として一鳥声きかず，木の下闇茂りあひ
て夜行くがごとし．雲端につちふる心地して，篠の中踏み分け
分け水をわたり岩に蹴いて，肌につめたき汗を流して最上の庄に
出づ．かの案内せし男の言ふやう「この道必ず不用の事あり．恙
なう送りまゐらせて仕合したりと，悦びて別れぬ．後に聞きてさ
へ胸とどろくのみなり．

🐑　尾花沢

尾花沢にて清風といふ者を尋ぬ。かれは富める者なれども、志いやしからず。都にも折々かよひて、さすがに旅の情をも知りたれば、日比とどめて長途のいたはりさまざまにもてなし侍る。

　　涼しさを我が宿にしてねまるなり

　　這ひ出でよ飼屋が下のひきの声

　　まゆはきを俤にして紅粉の花

　　蚕飼する人は古代の姿かな　　　　　　　曽良

🌙　立石寺

山形領に立石寺といふ山寺あり。慈覚大師の開基にして、殊に清閑の地なり。一見すべきよし人々のすすむるによりて、尾花沢よりとつて返し、その間七里ばかりなり。日いまだ暮れず。麓の坊に宿かり置きて、山上の堂にのぼる。岩に巌を重ねて山とし、松柏年旧り、土石老いて苔滑らかに、岩上の院々扉を閉ぢて物の音きこえず。岸をめぐり岩を這ひて仏閣を拝し、佳景寂莫として心

澄みゆくのみ覚ゆ.

閑さや岩にしみ入る蟬の声

大石田

最上川乗らんと，大石田といふ所に日和を待つ．ここに古き俳諧の種こぼれて，忘れぬ花の昔をしたひ，芦角一声の心をやはらげ，この道にさぐり足して新古ふた道に踏みまよふといへども，みちしるべする人しなければと，わりなき一巻残しぬ．このたびの風流ここに至れり．

最上川

最上川は，みちのくより出でて，山形を水上とす．碁点・隼などいふ恐しき難所あり．板敷山の北を流れて，果は酒田の海に入る．左右山覆ひ，茂みの中に船を下す．これに稲つみたるをや稲船といふならし．白糸の滝は青葉の隙々に落ちて，仙人堂岸に臨みて立つ．水みなぎつて舟あやふし．

五月雨をあつめて早し最上川

羽黒山

六月三日，羽黒山に登る．図司左吉といふ者を尋ねて，別当代会覚阿闍梨に謁す．南谷の別院に舎して憐憫の情こまやかにあるじせらる．

四日，本坊において俳諧興行．

ありがたや雪をかをらす南谷

五日，権現に詣づ．当山開闢能除大師は，いづれの代の人といふことを知らず．延喜式に「羽州里山の神社」とあり．書写，「黒」の字を「里山」となせるにや．羽州黒山を中略して羽黒山といふにや．出羽といへる は，「鳥の毛羽をこの国の 貢 に 献 る」と風土記に侍るとやらん．月山・湯殿を合せて三山とす．当寺武江東叡に属して，天台止観の月明らかに，円頓融通の法の 灯 かかげそひて，僧坊棟をならべ，修験行法を励まし，霊山霊地の験効，人貴び且つ恐る．繁栄 長 にしてめでたき御山と謂ひつべし．

🌙　月山・湯殿山

八日, 月山にのぼる. 木綿しめ身に引きかけ, 宝冠に頭を包み, 強力といふものに導かれて, 雲霧山気の中に氷雪を踏んで登ること八里, 更に日月行道の雲関に入るかとあやしまれ, 息絶え身こごえて頂上に到れば, 日没して月顕る. 笹を敷き篠を枕として, 臥して明くるを待つ. 日出でて雲消ゆれば湯殿に下る.

谷の傍に鍛治小屋といふあり. この国の鍛治, 霊水を撰びて, ここに潔斎して剣を打ち, 終に「月山」と銘を切つて世に賞せらる. かの龍泉に剣を淬ぐとかや, 干将・莫耶の昔をしたふ. 道に堪能の執あさからぬこと知られたり. 岩に腰かけてしばし休らふほど, 三尺ばかりなる桜のつぼみ半ばひらけるあり. 降り積む雪の下に埋れて春を忘れぬ遅桜の花の心わりなし. 炎天の梅花ここにかをるがごとし. 行尊僧正の歌の哀もここに思ひ出でて, なほまさりて覚ゆ. 惣じて, この山中の微細, 行者の法式として他言すること禁ず. よつて筆をとどめて記さず. 坊に帰れば, 阿闍梨の需めによりて, 三山順礼の句々短冊に書く.

　　涼しさやほの三日月の羽黒山

　　雲の峰幾つ崩れて月の山

　　語られぬ湯殿にぬらす袂かな

湯殿山銭ふむ道の泪かな　　　　　　　　曽良

酒田

羽黒を立ちて鶴が岡の城下，長山氏重行といふ武士の家に迎へら
れて，俳諧一巻あり．左吉もともに送りぬ．川舟に乗りて酒田の
湊に下る．淵庵不玉といふ医師のもとを宿とす．

あつみ山や吹浦かけて夕すずみ

暑き日を海に入れたり最上川

象潟

江山水陸の風光数を尽して，今象潟に方寸を責む．酒田の湊より
東北の方，山を越え磯を伝ひ，いさごを踏みて，その際十里，日
影やや傾くところ，汐風真砂を吹き上げ，雨朦朧として鳥海の山か
くる．闇中に摸索して，「雨もまた奇なり」とせば，雨後の晴色
また頼もしきと，蜑の苫屋に膝をいれて雨の晴るるを待つ．
その朝，天よく晴れて朝日花やかにさし出づるほどに，象潟に舟

をうかぶ．まづ能因島に舟をよせて，三年幽居の跡を訪ひ，むかうの岸に舟をあがれば，「花の上こぐ」と詠まれし楼の老木，西行法師の記念をのこす．江上に御陵あり，神功后宮の御墓といひ，寺を干満珠寺といふ．この所に行幸ありし事いまだ聞かず．いかなる事にや．

この寺の方丈に座して簾を捲げば，風景一眼の中に尽きて，南に鳥海天をささへ，その陰うつりて江にあり．西はむやむやの関路をかぎり，東に堤を築きて秋田にかよふ道遙かに，海北にかまへて波うち入るる所を汐越といふ．江の縦横一里ばかり，俤松島にかよひて，また異なり．松島は笑ふがごとく，象潟はうらむがごとし．寂しさに悲しみを加へて，地勢魂をなやますに似たり．

象潟や雨に西施が合歓の花

汐越や鶴はぎぬれて海涼し

　　祭礼

象潟や料理何くふ神祭　　　　　　　　　　　　　　　曽良

蜑の家や戸板を敷きて夕涼み　　　　　　　　　（美濃の国の商人）
　　　　　　　　　　　　　　　　　　　　　　　　　低耳

　　　岩上に雎鳩の巣を見る

波こえぬ契ありてやみさごの巣　　　　　　　　　曽良

酒田のなごり日を重ねて，北陸道の雲に望む．遙々の思ひ胸をいたましめて，加賀の府まで百三十里と聞く．鼠の関を越ゆれば越後の地に歩行を改めて，越中の国市振の関に到る．この間九日，暑湿の労に神をなやまし，病おこりて事をしるさず．

　　文 月 や 六 日 も 常 の 夜 に は 似 ず

　　荒 海 や 佐 渡 に よ こ た ふ 天 河

今日は親知らず・子知らず・犬戻・駒返などいふ北国一の難所を越えて，疲れ侍れば，枕引きよせて寝ねたるに，一間隔てて西の方に，若き女の声二人ばかりと聞ゆ．年老いたる男の声も交りて物語するを聞けば，越後の国新潟といふ所の遊女なりし．伊勢参宮するとて，この関まで男の送りて明日は古郷に返す文をしたためて，はかなき言伝などしやるなり．白波のよする汀に身をはふらかし，あまのこの世をあさましう下りて，定めなき契，日々の業因いかにつたなしと，物言ふを聞くきく寝入りて，あした旅立つに，我々にむかひて，「行方しらぬ旅路の憂さ，あまりおぼつかなう悲しく侍れば，見えがくれにも御跡をしたひ侍らん．衣の上の御情に大慈の恵をたれて結縁せさせ給へ」と泪を落す．「不便の事には侍れども，我々は所々にてとどまる方おほし．ただ人の行くにまかせて行くべし．神明の加護かならず恙なかるべし」

と言ひ捨てて出でつつ, 哀れさしばらくやまざりけらし.

　　一家に遊女もねたり萩と月

曽良に語れば, 書きとどめ侍る.

　🌙　那古浦

黒部四十八が瀬とかや, 数しらぬ川をわたりて那古といふ浦に出づ. 担籠の藤浪は春ならずとも, 初秋のあはれ訪ふべきものをと, 人に尋ぬれば, 「これより五里, 磯づたひしてむかうの山陰に入り, 蜑の苫ぶきかすかなれば芦の一夜の宿かす者あるまじ」と言ひおどされて, 加賀の国に入る.

　　早稲の香や分け入る右は有磯海

　☁️　金沢

卯の花山・くりからが谷を越えて, 金沢は七月中の五日なり. ここに大坂より通ふ商人何処といふ者あり. それが旅宿をともにす.

一笑といふ者は，この道に好ける名のほのぼの聞えて，世に知る人も侍りしに，去年の冬，早世したりとて，その兄追善を催すに，

塚 も 動 け 我 が 泣 く 声 は 秋 の 風

ある草庵にいざなはれて

秋 涼 し 手 ご と に む け や 瓜 茄 子

途中吟

あ か あ か と 日 は つ れ な く も 秋 の 風

小松といふ所にて

し を ら し き 名 や 小 松 吹 く 萩 す す き

多太神社

この所，多太の神社に詣づ．実盛が甲・錦の切あり．往昔，源氏に属せし時，義朝公より賜らせ給ふとかや．げにも平士のものにあらず．目庇より吹返まで菊唐草の彫りもの金をちりばめ，龍

116

頭に鍬形打つたり。実盛討死の後、木曽義仲願状に添へて、この社にこめられ侍るよし、樋口の次郎が使せし事ども、まのあたり縁起に見えたり。

　　むざんやな甲の下のきりぎりす

🐗　那谷寺

山中の温泉に行くほど、白根が岳跡に見なして歩む。左の山際に観音堂あり。花山の法皇三十三所の順礼とげさせ給ひて後、大慈大悲の像を安置し給ひて、那谷と名付給ふとなり。那智・谷汲の二字を分ち侍りしとぞ。奇石さまざまに、古松植ゑならべて、萱ぶきの小堂岩の上に造りかけて殊勝の土地なり。

　　石山の石より白し秋の風

🌙　山中温泉

温泉に浴す．その効有馬に次ぐといふ．

　　　山中や菊は手折らぬ湯の匂

あるじとする者は久米之助とて，いまだ小童なり．かれが父俳諧を好み，洛の貞室若輩の昔ここに来りし比，風雅に辱しめられて，洛に帰りて貞徳の門人となつて世に知らる．功名の後，この一材判詞の料を請けずといふ．今更昔語りとはなりぬ．
曽良は腹を病みて，伊勢の国長島といふ所にゆかりあれば，先立ちて行くに，

　　　行きゆきて倒れ伏すとも萩の原　　　　曽良

と書き置きたり．行く者の悲しみ残る者のうらみ，隻鳧の別れて雲に迷ふがごとし．予も又，

　　　今日よりや書付消さん笠の露

118

KODANSHA INTERNATIONAL PAPERBACKS ABOUT JAPAN

affordable,

absorbing,

and

growing...

全昌寺

大聖持の城外，全昌寺といふ寺にとまる．なほ加賀の地なり，曽良も前の夜，この寺に泊りて，

　　終宵秋風聞くや裏の山

と残す．一夜の隔千里に同じ．吾も秋風を聞きて衆寮に臥せば，あけぼのの空近う読経声澄むままに，鐘板鳴つて食堂に入る．今日は越前の国へと心早卒にして堂下に下るを，若き僧ども紙・硯をかかへ，階のもとまで追ひ来る．折節庭中の柳散れば，

　　庭掃いて出でばや寺に散る柳

とりあへぬさまして草鞋ながら書き捨つ．

永平寺入り

越前の境，吉崎の入江を舟に棹して汐越の松を尋ぬ．

　　終宵嵐に波をはこばせて

月 を た れ た る 汐<ruby>越<rt>こし</rt></ruby>の 松   西行

この一首にて数景尽きたり。もし一弁を加ふるものは，無用の指
を立つるがごとし。

丸岡天龍寺の長老，古き<ruby>因<rt>ちなみ</rt></ruby>あれば尋ぬ。また金沢の<ruby>北枝<rt>ほくし</rt></ruby>といふ者，
かりそめに見送りて，この所までしたひ来る。所々の風景<ruby>過<rt>すぐ</rt></ruby>さず
思ひつづけて，折節あはれなる<ruby>作意<rt>さくい</rt></ruby>など聞ゆ。今既に別れに<ruby>臨<rt>のぞ</rt></ruby>み
て，

物 書 き て <ruby>扇<rt>あふぎ</rt></ruby>引 き さ く な ご り か な

<ruby>五十丁山<rt>ごじふちやうやま</rt></ruby>に入りて<ruby>永平寺<rt>えいへいじ</rt></ruby>を<ruby>礼<rt>らい</rt></ruby>す。<ruby>道元禅師<rt>だうげんぜんじ</rt></ruby>の<ruby>御寺<rt>みてら</rt></ruby>なり。<ruby>邦畿<rt>はうき</rt></ruby>千里
を避けて，かかる山陰に跡を残し給ふも，<ruby>貴<rt>たふと</rt></ruby>きゆゑありとかや。

🐗 福井・敦賀

福井は三里ばかりなれば，<ruby>夕飯<rt>ゆふめし</rt></ruby>したためて出づるに，たそかれの
<ruby>路<rt>みち</rt></ruby>たどたどし。ここに等栽といふ古き<ruby>隠士<rt>いんじ</rt></ruby>あり。いづれの年に
か，江戸に<ruby>来<rt>きた</rt></ruby>りて予を尋ぬ。遙か<ruby>十年<rt>ととせ</rt></ruby>余りなり。いかに老いさら
ぼひてあるにや，はた死にけるにやと人に尋ね侍れば，いまだ存
命してそこそことを教ふ。市中ひそかに引き入りて，あやしの小家
に<ruby>夕顔<rt>ゆふがほ</rt></ruby>・へちまの<ruby>延<rt>は</rt></ruby>えかかりて，鶏頭・<ruby>帚木<rt>ははきぎ</rt></ruby>に戸ぼそをかくす。

さては，このうちにこそと門を扣けば，侘しげなる女の出でて，「いづくよりわたり給ふ道心の御坊にや．あるじは，このあたり何某といふ者の方に行きぬ．もし用あらば尋ね給へ」といふ．かれが妻なるべしと知らる．昔物語にこそかかる風情は侍れと，やがて尋ねあひて，その家に二夜とまりて，名目は敦賀の湊にと旅立つ．等栽もともに送らんと，裾をかしうからげて路の枝折と浮かれ立つ．

漸 白根が岳かくれて，比那が岳あらはる．あさむづの橋をわたりて，玉江の芦は穂に出でにけり．鶯の関を過ぎて湯尾峠を越ゆれば，燧が城，帰山に初鴈を聞きて，十四日の夕暮敦賀の津に宿を求む．

その夜，月殊に晴れたり．「明日の夜もかくあるべきにや」と言へば，「越路の習ひ，なほ明夜の陰晴はかりがたし」と，あるじに酒すすめられて，気比の明神に夜参す．仲哀天皇の御廟なり．社頭神さびて，松の木の間に月のもり入りたる，お前の白砂霜を敷けるがごとし．「往昔，遊行二世の上人大願発起の事ありて，みづから草を刈り土石を荷ひ，泥渟をかわかせて，参詣往来の煩なし．古例今に絶えず，神前に真砂を荷ひ給ふ．これを遊行の砂持と申し侍る」と亭主の語りける．

　　　月 清 し 遊 行 の 持 て る 砂 の 上

十五日，亭主の詞にたがはず雨降る．

　　　名 月 や 北 国 日 和 定 め な き

種の浜

十六日，空晴れたれば，ますほの小貝拾はんと種の浜に舟を走らす．海上七里あり．天屋何某といふ者，破籠・小竹筒などこまやかにしたためさせ，僕あまた舟にとりのせて，追風時のまに吹き着きぬ．

浜はわづかなる海士の小家にて，佗しき法華寺あり．ここに茶を飲み酒をあたためて，夕ぐれのさびしさ感に堪へたり．

　　寂 し さ や 須 磨 に 勝 ち た る 浜 の 秋

　　波 の 間 や 小 貝 に ま じ る 萩 の 塵

その日のあらまし等栽に筆をとらせて寺に残す．

122

🐚 大垣

露通もこの港まで出でむかひて，美濃の国へと伴ふ．駒にたすけ
られて大垣の庄に入れば，曽良も伊勢より来り合ひ，越人も馬を
とばせて如行が家に入り集る．前川子・荊口父子，そのほか親し
き人々日夜訪ひて，蘇生の者に会ふがごとく，且つ悦び且ついた
はる．
旅のもの憂さもいまだやまざるに　長月六日になれば，伊勢の遷
宮拝まんと，又舟にのりて，

　蛤のふたみにわかれ行く秋ぞ

✿ 跋

　からびたるも，艶たるも，たくましきも，はかなげなるも，奥
の細道見もてゆくに，おぼえず立ちて手たたき，伏してむらぎも
を刻む．一般はみのを着る着る，かかる旅せまほしと思ひ立ち，
一度は座して，まのあたり奇景をあまんず．かくて百般の情に鮫
人が玉を翰に示したり．旅なるかな，器なるかな．ただ嘆かはし
きは，かうやうの人のいとかよわげにて，眉の霜の置きそふぞ．

　　　　元禄七年初夏　　　　　　　　　　　素竜書

Now available in Kodansha International's new paperback series:

THE WAITING YEARS

FUMIKO ENCHI
Translated by John Bester

"The relationships of the women to each other...are portrayed with a delicacy and a discernment that reveal the author to be a woman of profound psychological insight."
—*Monumenta Nipponica*
204 pages

THE DARK ROOM

JUNNOSUKE YOSHIYUKI
Translated by John Bester

"Makes one convinced anew that Japanese literature is now definitely an integral part of world literature, not an isolated freak phenomenon prized only for its exotic quality. And the translation is superb."
—*Oriental Economist*
170 pages

NON-FICTION PAPERBACK TITLES

WAR CRIMINAL
The Life and Death of Hirota Koki

SABURO SHIROYAMA
Translated by John Bester

"Fluid, contemporary, and interspersed with the rich, true detail that gives dimension to history."
—*Business Japan*
"A brilliant, dispassionate account."
—*Fort Worth Star-Telegram*
301 pages

BLACK RAIN

MASUJI IBUSE
Translated by John Bester

"The most successful book yet written about the greatest single horror inflicted by one group of men upon another."
—*Julian Symons, Sunday Times*
300 pages

JAPAN'S LONGEST DAY
The Pacific War Research Society

"Few contemporary books give one such an insight into the traditions and values of prewar Japan....Japan's longest day...was full of tragedy and courage, but the spirit of those who experienced it did much to lay the foundation for the new Japan. This excellent book makes it possible to understand that spirit."
—*John M. Allison, United States Ambassador to Japan, 1953-57*
340 pages

OTHER TITLES:

Lou-lan and Other Stories
—*Yasushi Inoue*

Clara's Diary: An American Girl in Meiji Japan
—*Clara A. N. Whitney*

Mirror, Sword and Jewel: The Geometry of Japanese Life
—*Kurt Singer*

Japanese Religion
—*Agency for Cultural Affairs*